POLITICAL ISLAM IN THE INDIAN SUBCONTINENT: THE JAMAAT-I-ISLAMI

Centre de Sciences Humaines (Centre for Social Sciences and Humanities): Created in New Delhi in 1989 the CSH, is part of network of research centres of the French Ministry of Foreign Affairs. The Centre's research work is primarily oriented towards the study of issues concerning the contemporary dynamics of development in India and South Asia. The activities of the Centre are focused on four main themes, namely: Economic growth and sustainable development, International and regional relations, Institutional structures and political constructions of identity and Urban dynamics.

(Centre de Sciences Humaines, 2 Aurangzeb Road, New Delhi 110011, India - Tel: (91 11) 301 62 59/ 301 41 73 - Fax: (91 11) 301 84 80 - E-mail: public@csh-delhi.com - Website: http://www.csh-delhi.com)

Institute Français de Pondichéry (French Institute of Pondicherry): Created in 1955, the IFP is a multidisciplinary research and advanced educational institute. Major research works are focusing on Sanskrit and Tamil languages and literatures—in close collaboration with the *Ecole Française d'Extrême- Orient*—ecosystems, biodiversity and sustainability, dynamics of population and socio-economic development.

(Institute Français de Pondichéry, 11, Saint Louis Street, P.B. 33 Pondicherry 605 001 - Tel.: (91 413) 334 170/334 168 - Telex: 469224 FRAN-In, Fax: (91 413) 339 534 - E-mail: instfran@giasmd01.vsnl.net.in - Website: http: www.ifpindia. org)

Political Islam in the Indian Subcontinent: The Jamaat-i-Islami

FRÉDÉRIC GRARE

MANOHAR

CENTRE DE SCIENCES HUMAINES
2005

First published 2001
Reprinted 2005

ISBN 81-7304-404-X

Published by
Ajay Kumar Jain for
Manohar Publishers & Distributors
4753/23 Ansari Road, Daryaganj
New Delhi 110 002

Distributed in South Asia by
FOUNDATION BOOKS
4381/4, Ansari Road
Daryaganj, New Delhi 110 002
and its branches at Mumbai, Hyderabad,
Bangalore, Chennai, Kolkata

Typeset by
Kohli Print
Delhi 110 051

Printed at
Lordson Publishers Pvt Ltd
Delhi 110 007

Contents

Acknowledgements

This book is largely due to Arnaud d'Andurain who first oriented my research towards this field of study. The findings contained in this volume have been collected during several research trips conducted both in Europe and in the Indian subcontinent and I would like to thank the *Fonds National Suisse de la Recherche Scientifique* whose support has allowed me to conduct some of them.

I want to express my deep gratitude to Professors Gilbert Etienne, from the Graduate Institute of International Studies, and Amitabh Mattoo from Jawaharlal Nehru University, as well as Alexander Evans from King's College who have read the manuscript and whose precious comments have helped me improve it. The remaining mistakes are my sole responsibility.

I also want to thank Mrs. Saroj Butani and Mrs. P. Varma who respectively translated and edited the manuscript. Finally, it would not be fair not to mention that this book would not have appeared without the work and dedication of Uma Krishnan.

FRÉDÉRIC GRARE

1. Introduction

Political Islam, which has now become an important issue in international relations, has assumed, in the eyes of the public, a negative image apparently for two reasons. Its erruption on the international political arena is perceived as a regressive phenomenon, reminiscent of a supposedly outmoded era in which irrationality competed with violence. It is, moreover, almost systematically identified with terrorism, with the media adding to the growing confusion between Islam and Islamism. It is also often identified with extreme religious fervour, with groups claiming affiliation with Islamism becoming concretely involved in some of the conflicts which are the bane of our world today. Their supposed potential for destabilization, both within the Muslim states of which they are a part, as also within societies where Islam is not predominant, are a cause of worry to governments. These factors combine to strengthen each other with the result that, rightly or wrongly, Islamism is represented as being one of the perils endangering our world at the close of the century.

It is necessary, for the purpose of the present volume to define Islamism. Islamism can, indeed, not be reduced to religious fervour or to the extreme moral rigorism characteristic of the Taliban or be reduced to the recourse to violence. It is defined, essentially, in its relationship to politics and hence to the state, by its efforts towards the realization of a truly Muslim society. It cannot result from a simple accumulation of believers whatever be the degree of their personal religious practice. The confusion arises partly out of the fact that in Islamism the conquest of political power is justified by the will to impose the Sharia, the sole juridical basis of social relationships before which no other non-Islamic law can exist. It is this assumption which makes Islamism totalitarian. The traditionalists, on the other hand, concede that it is up to the Sharia to govern society but that does not prejudice, in any way, the nature of the political system which, while it must respect the value system of Islam, nevertheless enjoys a genuine autonomy.

Though this phenomenon has been partially examined by Western social scientists, they have confined themselves to its manifestations in the Arab and the Iranian worlds. Besides historical factors, the strategic importance of the region has made Western researchers turn greater attention to the events occurring in this area. Iran's Islamic revolution, the civil war in Algeria and the fragility, to say the least, of the Arab-Israel 'peace process', have further strengthened this trend. The Islamism of the Indian subcontinent, on the other hand, has till recently attracted the attention of the various media only insofar as it is a component of regional conflicts (Afghanistan and Kashmir), leading obviously to biases and distortions, depending on the more or less direct impact of the problem on the country in question. Generally speaking, social science researchers of the West have taken little interest till now in the Indian subcontinent, the third cultural centre of Islamism.

The present study aspires to contribute, in a modest way, towards filling these lacunae. Its point of focus is one particular movement, the Jamaat-i-Islami, whose history follows incisively that of the subcontinent but whose influence spills over well beyond its borders. Its founder, Abul Ala Mawdudi, who died in

1979, was one of the first and the most important among the theoreticians of political Islam. He is said to have had a great influence on Hassan el Banna, and on Sayyed Qotb, founders of the Egyptian Muslim Brothers. History, as also recent current events therefore, prompt one to examine the links of the Jamaat with other Islamist organizations throughout the world.

Set up in 1941, the Jamaat-i-Islami, under the impetus of its founder, initially opposed the creation of Pakistan, but later framed its entire strategy within the structure of the new state. It also experienced the same divisions that the subcontinent had been subjected to. It fell prey to a schism first during the partition of India in 1947, with the formation of an Indian branch and a Pakistani branch, and then a second split occurred at the time of the secession of Bangladesh. The Jamaat-i-Islami exists today under this name in five different regions. It is found in Pakistan, naturally, but also in India, in Jammu and Kashmir, in 'Azad Kashmir'[1] and in Bangladesh. A branch of the movement is also said to be located in Sri Lanka. The nature and the intensity of the bonds that may exist between the different components of the movement, therefore, need to be examined as also the extent to which they affect or are likely to affect the geopolitics of the region. The persistence of conflicts like those in Kashmir and Afghanistan and the possibility of seeing the Indian subcontinent turning into a zone of chronic instability are causes that call for a close study of the factors identified as being fraught with the possibility of leading to an implosion.

This brief analysis will, however, concern itself for the larger part with the Pakistani Jamaat-i-Islami. This movement is, in fact, most powerful in Pakistan and it is there that its action is most deeply woven into the political life of the country and is most visible. It is also from Pakistan, and sometimes with its support, that its activity is deployed towards the trouble spots of the subcontinent and beyond. At the same time, it influences in a significant manner the perception of Pakistan by the outside world, which is very often out of proportion to its real influence.

The present study aims at analysing the working of the movement and its will and capacity to influence events, both in the Indian subcontinent as well as outside it. It attempts to examine its plan of work, its organization and its policies, as also to identify its networks in order to highlight its actual sphere of influence. It thus aspires to bring out the regional and international strategies of the Jamaat and to underscore thereby the points of convergence as well as the limits to the cooperation between Islamist movements. It then tries to uncover the mechanisms through which the Pakistani authorities make use of the Jamaat to promote their regional interests, particularly in Kashmir and Afghanistan, as also the way in which Pakistan's rivals, India particularly, make use of these same mechanisms to bring disparagement to Pakistan. By doing so it aims to highlight the links between the state and religious groups as well as the ambiguous relationship forged through reciprocal instrumentalization prevailing between state authorities and Islamist movements. Through the study of the Jamaat-i-Islami this research hopes to explain how a specific religious group can support the objectives of a political system by acting as a 'torch bearer of irredentist ambitions'.[2]

Finally, though incidentally, through a case study, the present research proposes to demonstrate that in spite of their pan-Islamic rhetoric, supposedly in response to the identity crisis prevailing in their societies of origin, most Islamist movements are themselves in a state of crisis. Torn as they are between being national political parties struggling for the conquest of power within a given political system and that of being part of the Islamist movement, a component of the international Islamic macrocosm, struggling to achieve the realization of an ideal, and to a certain extent an a-geographic, Muslim community, they are themselves searching for an identity and an idealogy. The choice between one or the other identity will not only have a direct incidence on the allocation of resources and hence on the effectiveness of the strategies adopted but will also constitute the key to the relations between Islamism and the West, giving them their real significance.

This dialectics, which determines the transition from Islamism, defined as consequence and integration of the national factor,[3] to neo-fundamentalism, does not constitute the affirmation of an implacable cultural opposition between two radically foreign worlds, but demonstrates on the contrary their falling within common conceptual categories (state, globalization), including their acceptance, rejection or more simply the difficulty in adapting to each of them. In the first case, the state is 'the constituent to which the universal has been attributed' and the sole 'authority for the establishment of social mores'. In the second case, all religious matters are reduced to an a-cultural and therefore potentially universal juridical code.

This, in the view of the author, is the perspective from which what has commonly come to be known as the 'Islamist peril', needs to be examined and which quite often only serves, in the West, as a guise to mask the resentment against immigration from the Muslim countries. In the Indian subcontinent, particularly in India, this same 'peril' serves both to demonize the neighbouring country of Pakistan and to constitute an element in the strategy of the marginalization of this latter country. It also crystallizes, in a more widely distributed and unacknowledged manner, as mistrust towards a Muslim minority constantly suspected of being a sort of fifth column of the 'land of the pure'. In both cases, moreover this sense of peril seems often justified by the terrorist attacks conducted by certain groups. The comparison between India and Europe appears to us to be all the more relevant as Islam is in both regions in the minority. It also leads one to speculate, at the time of incidents such as the 'Rushdie Affair', over the influence, both potential and real, of Islamist movements such as the Jamaat, on these minorities.

As the sources available are sparse, with the exception of texts by Mawdudi which are widely disseminated, this work is based mostly on field investigations conducted in Pakistan naturally, but also in Afghanistan, India, Bangladesh and the United Kingdom. An attempt has also been made to meet most of the national and regional leaders of the Jamaat-i-Islami. The wide geographic canvas makes it possible to place the Jamaat-i-Islami in its proper perspective while distinguishing two different modes of functioning, depending on whether it is deployed in Muslim majority countries or in countries where Islam is, on the contrary, in a minority. This distinction is linked with the distinction, conceptual in nature, between Islamic nationalism and neo-fundamentalism. This, in our view, seems also to constitute the originality of the present work. By viewing the Jamaat through its sole rhetoric or its organization, one runs the risk of endowing it with an influence that it does not possess and of thus bestowing on it an image of power which it utilizes in turn to legitimize and reinforce its role. It is only by viewing it in the historical perspective, combined with a strategic analysis of regional factors, that one can put into perspective the real impact of the Jamaat in Pakistan's political life and bring out its margins of manoeuvre. It constitutes, at the same time, its limits, the work losing in historical depth what it gains in geographical expanse.

The attempt, in this study will be to integrate these different approaches in order to determine as best as one can the dynamics of the movement and to make known its limits. It aims at contributing, however, modestly, towards the analysis of the political sociology of Pakistan, as also towards putting into proper perspective the Islamic character of the 'land of the pure'. If it is often repeatedly said, though without great discernment, that Pakistan was created in the name of Islam, it is due largely to the Jamaat. Pakistan is undoubtedly the only country whose history, despite its inevitably being a constellation of economic, social, cultural, political and other factors, is studied from the single angle of Islam. That Pakistan came into being as a result of the feeling of economic insecurity of the Muslims of the subcontinent, that the 'freedom movement' was a reflection of the aspirations of the Muslims in many aspects of their individual and collective lives and that the demography of the Muslims on the eastern and western wings of the subcontinent was a final and decisive factor are elements that are most often drowned in the din of the slogans of the Muslim League alone.[4] Now, while it is true that the founding fathers of Pakistan made use of religion to mobilize public opinion, this utilization of religion for political ends also arose partly out of tactical necessities. It was in this context that the entire political action of Mawdudi and of the Jamaat was deployed. It was, in fact, his relentless campaign for an Islamic constitution, a campaign which he undertook as soon as the new state was constituted, which maintained, and continues to maintain even today Islam in the foreground of Pakistan's political scene. But in the process, the Jamaat did 'nationalize' itself as much as the Pakistani state was 'Islamized'.

This study attempts to analyse, in each of the spheres of activity of the Jamaat, the elements relating to its doctrine as well as to examine their implementation on the ground, while situating them in their context. Tracing the history of the involvement of the Jamaat-i-Islami in Pakistani politics, it notes that it has only met with failure. More than fifty years after its creation, the Jamaat-i-Islami has still not succeeded in coming into power in Pakistan in spite of the repeated assertions of its leaders that power would inevitably come into their hands at the end of a period which they invariably assess as five years. Similarly, its pan-Islamist project appears today to have run out of steam. This study, therefore, attempts to determine the reasons for this failure by analysing both the plans of the Jamaat and the social, political and strategic conditions of their implementation. Proceeding by way of concentric circles, the initial part of this study is devoted to the analysis of the involvement of the Jamaat in Pakistan's internal policy. The second part deals with its influence in matters of external policy and the last part attempts to achieve a better understanding of the exact nature of its relations with the West.

Finally, it is necessary to specify what the present study is not. The following lines do not pretend to teach anybody, specially the Muslims, what the 'true Islam' is all about, nor to assess whether the ideology of the Jamaat corresponds to such a hypothetical definition. The author has neither the competence, nor the willingness to do so. His purpose is simply to examine and analyse the role of a prominent Islamist party, the Jamaat-i-Islami, as an actor in the social, political and strategic fields. The perspective is therefore totally a-religious. It must be acknowledged also that the formulations of Olivier Roy and Jean-François Meyer and their work on political Islam and fundamentalism have incontestably constituted the thread of this study.

NOTES

1. Literally, Free Kashmir. This phrase refers, in fact, to that part of Kashmir which is controlled by Pakistan. Indians use the expression 'Pakistan Occupied Kashmir' (POK).
2. Jean-Francois Mayer, *Religions et sécurité internationale*, Berne: Central Defence Office, December 1995.
3. Olivier Roy , 'Le néo-fondamentalisme islamique ou l'imaginaire de l'oummah', *Esprit*, April 1996, pp. 80–107, specially p. 82.
4. Ibid., p. 86.
5. Muhammad Aslam Syed (ed.), *Islam and Democracy in Pakistan*, Islamabad: National Institute of Historical and Cultural Research, 1995, p. 2.

2. Early Stages: In Search of an Ideology

BIRTH OF THE JAMAAT-I-ISLAMI

The history of the Jamaat-i-Islami is closely linked to that of its founder, Abul Ala Mawdudi. He was born in Hyderabad in 1903, and although self-taught, quickly became a prolific author. He is often considered to be one of the foremost figures of Islam in the twentieth century. A gifted orator, excellent organizer and charismatic leader, he was to leave his imprint on political Islam and influence a large number of his contemporaries, particularly Sayyed Qotb, an outstanding personality and the main ideologist of the Egyptian Muslim Brothers.

Mawdudi[1] began his public career in 1920 when, at the age of seventeen, he became the chief editor of the Urdu weekly *Taj*. He then headed several newspapers and journals till he was appointed, in 1923, the editor of the monthly *Tarjuman al Quran*. In 1938 he was briefly appointed Dean of the Faculty of Theology of Islamya College but he returned to his former post less than a year later and never left it thereafter. It was in

1927, however, that he published his first two works, *Al-Jihad Fil Islam* and *Dawlat Arafya va Hukumat-i-Bartanwa*. But it was *Towards understanding Islam*, published in 1933, which was to turn him into one of the very first Indian theologians. Initially written in Urdu, the work was translated into English and recommended for use in all religious schools as soon as it was published. Thereafter, Mawdudi continued incessantly to write and travel throughout the country to spread his teachings among Muslims all over India.

The Jamaat-i-Islami was founded in Lahore on 26 August 1941. It was not by chance that this place was chosen. It was in Lahore that Jinnah had launched, a year earlier, the famous 'Lahore resolution' in which he had called for the formation of Pakistan. Mawdudi, for his part, had been prophesying for several years that the civilization of his time, which was represented, to his mind by capitalism, socialism and fascism, was leading the world to its doom.[2] Islam alone seemed to him to be capable of taking humanity out of the darkness into which it had fallen. Ideology alone was, however, not enough. He needed an instrument likely to promote it, and at the proper time, to put it into practice. Hence the necessity for a party.

In response to an advertisement in the *Tarjuman al Quran* seventy-five persons met at Islamia Park in Lahore on 26 August 1941. There Mawdudi delivered a speech during which he announced the main objectives of his organization. He affirmed notably:

- that while the other movements remained content with incorporating some parts of Islam or some objectives accepted by all Muslims, the objective of the Jamaat was to promote Islam in its totality; that the Jamaat would adopt the same system of organization as adopted by the Prophet;
- that ultimately the Jamaat would not restrict its activities to Indian Muslims alone but would appeal to Muslims the world over.[3]

With this the Jamaat was born. From the outset, however, the political climate which then prevailed in India presented organizational problems for the party which could not meet as easily and as freely as it would have liked to do. What is more, it was also out of tune with the larger trends which were then emerging in the life of the country. Analysing the Indian situation, Mawdudi noted that 'the various nationalities were now out to annihilate each other'.[4] By nationality he meant, in fact, religious kinship, thus indirectly supporting Jinnah's idea that it was religion which constituted the basis of nationality. Consequently he held the 'nationalism' of the Hindus, the Sikhs and the Muslims as being responsible for the communal riots which had broken out before Partition.

At the same time, he denounced the secularism of the Congress for being irreligious and because he had no faith in its objective of establishing a united and independent India. He felt that democracy meant the rule of the majority, in this case of the Hindus and therefore the subjugation of the Muslims. Hence, he condemned Muslim nationalism for having accepted the principle of the rule of the majority over an oppressed minority in the two zones where the Hindus and the Muslims respectively were in the majority. As he saw it, no nation state could tolerate within itself the existence of another nationality having distinct national demands. Three possibilities were, therefore, open to Indian Muslims. These could either accept the policy of nationalist Muslims and get absorbed into the Hindu majority or continue to follow the policy of Muslim nationalism and be annihilated or give up the path of nationalism and concentrate on 'the call of Islam'.[5]

Events, however, overtook him rapidly. On 15 August 1947 the Indian empire gave birth to two independent states, India and Pakistan. Mawdudi emigrated to Lahore. The Jamaat-i-Islami experienced the full force of Partition and was divided into two organizations, the Jamaat-i-Islami Pakistan and the Jamaat-i-Islami Hind. A new chapter was written in the history of the movement.

IDEOLOGY: MAWDUDI AND THEODEMOCRACY

Mawdudi formulated most of his ideology during the years preceding Partition. Since most of the ethical and theological concepts around which his political thought revolved were formulated between 1920 and Partition in 1947, he did not have any directly political objectives at the time. His concept of the Islamic state remained, during this period therefore, essentially theoretical.

The central idea around which Mawdudi's political thought revolves is that of the transcendence of religious law. 'There is only one single law, the Sharia, imposed from above by God who is the only lawmaker and the only sovereign.'[6] This concept of a 'divine sovereign' is central to his thought. It constitutes, according to Mawdudi, the main difference between the Islamic political system and Western democracy in which sovereignty belongs to the people. For him, 'every notion of our absolute independence is nothing but a sheer deception and misjudgement. God controls every fibre of our being and none can escape His grip.'[7] Indeed, 'firstly, the power and the organs through which our free-will functions, are a gift from God and not the result of our own efforts; secondly, the independence of choice itself has been delegated to us by God and not by us through our personal endeavour; thirdly, all those things in which our free-will operates are not only the property but also the creation of God; fourthly, the territory in which we exercise our independence and freedom is also the territory of God'.[8] In Mawdudi's conception, to acknowledge any other entity as being sovereign or to accept any other principle of authority is equivalent to idolatry.[9] It follows from this that no legislation can ever be made without taking religion into account. Even in those fields on which the Koran and the Sunnah are silent the laws promulgated should conform to the general principles expounded by the Sharia, which cannot be modified.[10] This latter must, therefore, become the law of the country and be applied to the fields of civil, penal and constitutional law.

Mawdudi was quick to realize the ideological significance of the notion of the unity and the indivisibility of divine sovereignty. In his view, it is this which gives to the world its meaning. The value of every human action resides in its degree of rectitude and goodness in the light of the highest values. The implementation of this value in concrete human action enables divine will to penetrate into the socio-political world.[11]

As mentioned earlier, Mawdudi's ideology stems from a dialectical concept of history. It opposes Islam to all that is 'non Islam' and the struggle between the two must inevitably culminate in an Islamic revolution and in the creation of an Islamic state which will initiate in society large scale reforms leading to a utopian Islamic order. In his view, the inevitable success of the Islamic state will necessarily strengthen its legitimacy.[12] But, as Nasr writes, 'it was obvious to Mawdudi that the Islamic state would not be able to reconcile the rigid demands of Islamic law and the ideals of democracy unless the population would willingly abide by the demands of Islamic law'.[13] It follows from this that it is necessary to Islamize society before creating the state, hence the stress laid by the Jamaat on education and propaganda.

The form of government of an Islamic state can be described as 'theodemocracy', based on the doctrine of the democratic Khalifat. Allah having made man his Khalif on earth it follows that man has the right only to exercise a power delegated to him and that this 'vice regency' of God is the collective law of all those who accept his absolute sovereignty and follow the precepts of the Sharia.[14] Theodemocracy can therefore be defined as 'a limited people's sovereignty under the suzerainty of God'.[15]

It is on this level that, for Mawdudi, the necessity for political power comes in. The reforms that Islam aspires to implement being impossible through predication and persuasion alone, it becomes necessary to make use of an authority having powers of coercion. But it is precisely here that the question of democracy once again reasserts itself, for what is to happen to non-Muslim minorities in an Islamic state? Besides, the Islamic state is necessarily a democratic state, not on account of its ability to incorporate various social interests but because divisions arising out of socio-economic disparities cannot exist within it.

THE JAMAAT-I-ISLAMI AND THE ISSUE OF THE NATION

Marc Gaborieau maintains that the 'two-nation theory' was above all the expression of a political strategy. 'The Muslims, who formed only 24% of the population of British India could not but be a minority without power in a unified independent India. The only way in which they could take their destiny in their own hands was by creating an autonomous Muslim state.'[16] But for Mawdudi, who desired first of all to reconstruct the religious thought of Islam, there was no historical basis for the belief that 'once you create a national Muslim state . . . you can convert it into an Islamic State through education, training and reform'.[17] He, consequently, invited Muslims to turn away from nationalism in all its forms and to accept the sole guidance of Islam which prohibits all sectarian interests, thus remaining faithful to a much more traditional notion of the unitary Muslim community, irrespective of country, language, nation or race.

Indeed, for Mawdudi, the concept of nationalism was an irrational one which destroyed the deeper bonds between individuals, divided humanity into racial groups, set up barriers of languages and demarcated artificial geographical borders.[18] In *Unity of the Muslim World*, Mawdudi clarifies by saying that 'One could scarcely conceive of the collective life of a nation except in terms of its being free and independent, its members being virtual worshippers of their nation, exerting themselves to the utmost to going for its glory and supremacy over all other nations even if that implied suppressing others and bringing other nations low.'[19] Nationalism, in his perception, had led, in the course of time, to catastrophes and world wars.[20] It was, therefore, basically incompatible with Islam. Mawdudi noted, moreover, that nationalism was a western concept which divided the Muslim world and thus promoted the supremacy of Western imperialist powers. Just a few months before partition, Mawdudi was to declare, 'why should we foolishly waste our time in expecting the so-called Muslim national state and fritter away our energies in setting it up, when we know that it will not only be useless for our purpose but will rather prove an obstacle in our path'.[21]

This attitude was not, however, the fruit of ideological arguments alone. It can be explained also by the conditions which prevailed when the Jamaat-i-Islami was formed. From the outset, the party had to distance itself from the Muslim League, the main Muslim party in India and which was then the advocate of the idea of a Muslim nation to be called Pakistan. The Jamaat-i-Islami could only distinguish itself from the latter by attacking both its project as well as its Islamic nature. As compared to the later evolution of the party and of its founder, it can be argued that, in spite of Mawdudi's writings, this opposition was due less to a negation in principle of the idea of the nation than to the secular character of the new state. If he reproached the latter with promoting the secular idea of a nation, it was basically because it replaced the religious notion of law.[22] Now, 'being devoid of the attributes of justice and of infallibility, the secular State can neither establish the rule of justice within its own borders with relation to the different classes of its subjects, nor act justly towards the people outside its domains'.[23] Hence war, tyranny and injustice. For Mawdudi, the remedy lay entirely in the acceptance of the doctrine of the sovereignty of God and the supremacy of the divine law in all spheres of life.[24] He also accused the leaders of the Muslim League of possessing neither religious knowledge nor the required uprightness and of being too Westernized to guide the Muslim community.

Once Partition had been carried about, the Jamaat deployed

its entire strategy within the framework of the Pakistani nation state and continued constantly to attempt to Islamize it. Acting, in spite of their initial reticence, within a legalistic framework, Mawdudi and the Jamaat launched a campaign for the establishment of Pakistan as an Islamic state. This was the starting point of the acceptance of the principle of nationhood. By agreeing to act within the legalistic framework of Pakistan, they also agreed to restrict themselves to a single country whose national characteristics they ended up by acknowledging. Pan-Islamist aspirations gave way, bit by bit and not without some reluctance, to political reality. Mawdudi drew, thereafter, a subtle distinction between secular nationalism, leading inevitably to a merciless struggle between states and Islamic nationalism, necessarily exempt from this type of conduct since it was meant to establish divine power on earth. This was not, however, without ambiguity since Islamic nationalism, which aimed at being the vector of the establishment of a universal Muslim community was, by this very fact, the bearer of its own negation. He, thus, declared in 1968, 'since by God's will, I was born in this particular nation and belong to it, it is but natural for me to wish and pray that my nation should have the proud privilege of leading the Islamic revolution in the present age, of being the first of the nations to adopt Islam in its totality, and to set up a model Islamic society which should serve as an example and a beacon for the rest of mankind'.[25] It would, therefore, not be an exaggeration to assert that the division in 1947 between what became the Pakistani branch of the movement and the originating branch, the Jamaat-i-Islami Hind, was more than a simple functional cleavage, without ideological repercussions. It was, indeed, a veritable split from which some very different trends were going to branch out: Islamo-nationalism on the one hand and neo-fundamentalism on the other. True, there was never a complete break between the two trends of the movement, for a meeting point was found in the theological bases of the Mawdudist ideology, but the differences surfaced thereafter each time the parties had to give their opinion on matters involving the national interests of their respective states, thus undermining implicitly the myth of a Muslim community overstepping, and even transcending, national borders.

On the surface, however, it is difficult to gauge, because of the common name they bear, anything other than straightforward alliance in the various branches of the Jamaat-i-Islami. They originate without doubt from a common nucleus, the Jamaat-i-Islami Hind, and constitute local branches of the party born out of the successive secessions of the Indian subcontinent. Their structures and their social bases,[26] also, are undoubtedly strictly identical. Their policies on the other hand, differ considerably. In a Muslim majority environment, their action tends to evolve always towards what Olivier Roy calls Islamo-nationalism. In countries where Islam is in a minority, however, they remain faithful to the initial 'revivalism' advocated by Mawdudi. This is the case, particularly with the Jamaat-i-Islami Hind, which will be dealt with later.

NOTES

1. For more on Mawdudi's life and work see, Reza Nasr Vali, 'Mawdudi and the Jama'at-i-Islami: The Origins, Theory and Practice of Islamic Revivalism', in Ali Rahnema (ed.), *Pioneers of Islamic Revival*, London: Zed Books, 1994, pp. 98–124.
2. Kalim Bahadur, *The Jama'at-i-Islami of Pakistan: Political Thought and Political Action*, New Delhi: Chetana Publications, 1979, p. 13.
3. See Kalim Bahadur, ibid., pp.13--15.
4. Ibid., p. 23.
5. Ibid.
6. Marc Gaborieau, 'Le néo-fondamentalisme au Pakistan: Maududi et la Jamaat-i-islami', in Olivier Carre and Paul Dumont, *Radicalismes islamiques*, Paris: l' Harmattan, 1986, p. 45.
7. S. Abul Ala Mawdudi, *Islamic Law and Constitution*, Lahore: Islamic Publications, 9th edn., June 1986, p. 47.
8. Ibid., p. 48.

9. Elisa Giunchi, 'The Political Thought of Abul A'La Mawdudi', *Il Politico*, April–June 1994, pp. 347–75, specially p. 352.
10. Ibid., p. 353.
11. See S.M.A. Sayyed, *The Myth of Authenticity: A Study of Islamic Fundamentalism*, Karachi: Royal Book Company, 1995, p. 190.
12. Sayyed Vali Reza Nasr, 'Mawdudi and the Jamaat-i-Islami: The Origins, Theory and Practice of Islamic Revivalism', in Rahnema Ali, *Pioneers of Islamic Revival*, London: Zed Books, 1994, pp. 98–124, specially p. 106.
13. Ibid., p. 107.
14. Ishtiaq Ahmed, *The Concept of an Islamic state in Pakistan*, Lahore: Vanguard, 1991, p. 98.
15. Quoted in Elisa Giunchi, op. cit., p. 353.
16. Marc Gaborieau, op. cit., pp. 33–76, specially p. 39.
17. M.S. Agwani, *Islamic Fundamentalism in India*, Chandigarh: Twenty-First Century India Society, 1986, p. 60.
18. On this subject see also Sayyed Abbas Aragghchi, 'Islamic Theo-Democrary: The Political Ideas of Abul A'La Mawdudi', *The Iranian Journal of International Affairs*, Vol. VIII, No. 4, Winter 1996–7, p. 790.
19. S. Abul Ala Mawdudi, *Unity of the Muslim World*, Lahore: Islamic Publications Ltd., 1st edn., July 1967, p. 1.
20. See S. Abul Ala Mawdudi, ibid.
21. Quoted in Elisa Giunchi, 'The Political Thought of Abul A'La Mawdudi', *Il Politico*, 1994, Anno LIX, No. 2, pp. 347–75, specially p. 358.
22. Marc Gaborieau, op. cit., p. 52.
23. M.S. Agwani, op. cit., p. 67.
24. Cf. Chap. 1 of this volume.
25. Quoted in Sayyed Abbas Araghchi, op. cit., p. 791.
26. With the exception of the Jamaat-i-Islami of Jammu & Kashmir, whose members come mostly from rural circles, all recruit their members from the highly educated urban lower/middle class.

3. The Jamaat-i-Islami in Pakistan Politics: The Improbable Advance towards Power

ENTRY ON THE POLITICAL STAGE

To arrive at an understanding of the Jamaat-i-Islami, it is necessary to once again retrace the intellectual evolution of its founder, Mawdudi. Careful not to get too closely involved in the pre-Partition political agitation and intent on 'reconstructing the religious thought of Islam',[1] he had from the outset opposed the 'movement for Pakistan'. His opposition was determined partly by his concept of history. The contours of the ideology of Mawdudi were indeed chalked out largely in a dialogue with Marxism and fascism, with the avowed intention of supplanting them. In the manner of Marxism, his ideology stemmed from a dialectical concept of history, the struggle between Islam and 'non-Islam' replacing the struggle between the classes as the central force of the historical progression of Muslim societies. According to Mawdudi, 'the struggle between Islam and non-Islam would culminate in an Islamic revolution and the creation of an Islamic state which would in turn initiate large scale reforms in society thereby leading to an utopian Islamic Order'.[2] Conversely, the success of the Islamic state would inevitably strengthen its legitimacy in the eyes of society. It followed from this that it was logically necessary to Islamize society prior to the creation of the state.[3]

But if Mawdudi was opposed to the creation of the new state, it was less on account of an opposition in principle[4] than because it was clear to him that Jinnah had no intention of making Pakistan an Islamic state. However, the latter did contribute, in no small measure, towards forming the political thought of the fundamentalist leader. It showed him, to begin with, the potential of religion in politics. For Mawdudi, the appropriation of religious symbols by the Muslim League, an appropriation crowned with success, proved indeed that Islam constituted the ultimate source of power and legitimacy among the Muslim community.[5] It blinded him, however, to the importance of socio-economic factors in the development of the 'movement for Pakistan'.

Mawdudi and the Jamaat-i-Islami got involved in the political life of Pakistan only very gradually, between 1948 and 1958 and they persistently played the role of an opponent. The initial ideological rigidity was replaced, over a period of time, by a greater pragmatism. Gradually, a distinct political ideology was formulated even as the Islamic vision was somewhat modified to include in it a commitment towards democracy and constitutional rights. With this, the Jamaat managed to infuse religious references into the Pakistani political discourse. The Jamaat, along with the overall assemblage of religious parties, came to constitute a distinct group of interests having specific demands with relation to the state but without the bond between the latter and Islam ever being strengthened.

It was, in fact, much more the Jamaat which was influenced by the creation of the Pakistani state than vice versa. The Jamaat was indeed quick to understand that without some support from the conservative ulemas, the army and the bureaucracy, its objective of establishing an Islamic state could not be realized. It had, therefore, to rethink its political strategy and to make compromises with those who, at least from a theoretical point of view, favoured the ideal of an Islamic system. Though it did not modify its ideology, its immediate political objective, namely to take the state machinery under its control, often got the better of the principle of ideological purity. The Jamaat quickly ceased to be an 'Islamic organization', a revivalist religious movement, to transform itself into a typical political party.[6]

THE FIRST STEP: THE DEBATE ON THE NATURE OF THE PAKISTANI STATE

Seeking to demonstrate the duplicity of the Muslim League in its call to Islam, the Jamaat began to demand, right from the month of December 1947, an increased Islamization of Pakistan. While Mawdudi had indeed, albeit unwillingly, accepted the creation of Pakistan he felt that the sole reason for its existence was to demonstrate the effectiveness of the Islamic way of life. The League seemed to him to have confined itself to the territorial concept of state. The contradiction stood out clearly on the question of Kashmir. India and Pakistan had, in fact, arrived in April 1948, at a ceasefire agreement by which each party undertook, among other things, to put an end to hostilities. However, 'covert' activities had not ceased from the Pakistani side. In a letter to Maulana Shabbir Ahmad Uthmani, the senior-most of the Pakistani *ulama*, Mawdudi declared that whatever be the intrinsic value of the agreement, it was binding on the Pakistani government and its citizens and that they were obliged by the Sharia to respect the terms of any agreement to which they were a party. Under these conditions, the carrying out of covert operations constituted a violation of the Sharia and consequently attested to the non-Islamic nature of Pakistan.[7]

This event was, however, one of the factors which was to prompt Mawdudi to show greater ideological resilience.

Rumours began to circulate over the content of this letter which was interpreted in some circles as a fatwa against jehad in Kashmir. Asked to explain his stand, Mawdudi replied that as long as Pakistan was bound by the terms of the ceasefire agreement, it could not declare jehad in Kashmir without at the same time violating the prescriptions of the Sharia. To Mawdudi, this did not in any way mean that Pakistan had given up its claim to Kashmir. But, keeping the Islamic nature of the state in mind he insisted that the latter should adhere to Islamic behaviour by officially denouncing the ceasefire agreement and hence resuming hostilities openly. His position was, however, greatly weakened by Indian propaganda which made use of his remarks to attempt to dampen the resolve of the Mujahideen. Mawdudi then began to be accused by the Pakistani government of sedition and disloyalty towards the 'movement for Pakistan'. He had, therefore, to modify his position by declaring his allegiance to Pakistan, denouncing India's politics and reaffirming the legitimacy of Pakistan's claims each time it intervened in Kashmir. He also accepted thereafter that volunteers could fight in Kashmir on the basis of an individual commitment, the Pakistani government remaining bound by the agreements signed with India. As soon as the government officially admitted its commitment to the conflict, he hastened to declare his support to jehad, in order to demonstrate the logic of his position.[8]

In August of the same year, a second incident found the Jamaat at loggerheads with the government, demonstrating once again the chasm between their respective concepts over the nature of Pakistan. Asked to comment on the question of the oath of allegiance to the state, Mawdudi replied that it was to God alone that a Muslim owed allegiance and that consequently, till Pakistan became an Islamic state, governed solely by the rules of the Sharia, he was prohibited from taking an oath of allegiance, and even more from serving in a non-Islamic entity, the Pakistani army.[9] The government reacted by immediately banning the publications of the Jamaat, particularly the

Tarjuman ul-Koran, while twenty-five members or sympathizers of the party were dismissed from the administration.[10] Mawdudi himself was arrested and imprisoned from October 1948 till the end of 1949. This incident, had a twofold significance for the leaders of the Jamaat. It showed them clearly the limits within which they would be allowed to act, limits which Mawdudi had crossed without, it would seem, even being aware of it, but it also underscored the reach of the Jamaat. They tried, thereafter, to act within these two parameters and obtained an initial victory in March 1949 when the Constituent Assembly adopted the principles of the future constitution which recognized the principle of divine sovereignty alone and the fact that the sovereignty of the state was but a delegated sovereignty: 'The sovereignty over the entire universe belongs to God Almighty alone, and the authority which he has delegated to the State of Pakistan through its people for being exercised within the limits prescribed by him is a sacred trust.'[11]

Relations with the government, it is true, improved significantly only after the death, in October 1951, of Liaquat Ali Khan. Several friends of Mawdudi thereafter became members of the government. The Jamaat had, however, understood, during this brief confrontation with the army that its salvation lay in safeguarding democracy. It, therefore, entered headlong into the struggle for a democratic constitution mixed with Islamic precepts, its growing influence enabling it to obtain some formal concessions in the text of the constitution ratified on 29 February 1956 by the Constituent Assembly. Pakistan, thus, became the 'Islamic Republic of Pakistan' and every legislative decision had thereafter to be subjected to 'Clause 205' which stipulated that no law contrary to the teachings of the Koran and the Hadiths could be adopted by Parliament.[12]

The period between 1947 and 1958 marked the entry of the Jamaat-i-Islami in the political life of Pakistan. It was after the promulgation of the constitution in 1958 that it took the final decision to enter into parliamentary politics. It took the plunge in 1957, during the preparation for the general elections provided for in the brand new constitution. During a particularly stormy general conference of the party, Mawdudi argued that the Jamaat had to enter into the political arena as this was the only way in which they could change the government and its leaders. A dissident faction, which wanted the Jamaat to remain a purely religious organization, found itself in a minority. Most of its members resigned.[13]

This change of strategy was to later influence considerably the very nature of the party's activism. It did, indeed, to a great extent camouflage its totalising, and even in many respects, totalitarian[14] ideology, in favour of a truly democratic discourse and practice since this became a condition of its political survival. It is this that, for a long time, marked the perception of the party in public opinion in Pakistan.

1958–1971, THE ARMY IN POWER: FROM IDEOLOGY TO PRAGMATISM

During the years of martial law (1958–62) the Jamaat-i-Islami was outlawed, as were other political institutions. Religious parties felt they were being specially targeted by the strike of the Pakistani generals. Under the army chiefs the Generals Ayub Khan (1958–69) and Yahya Khan (1969–71) this trend was further strengthened. The members of the Jamaat interpreted Ayub Khan's coup, particularly, as an attempt to eliminate any possibility of an electoral victory by Islamic parties by suppressing the 1956 constitution. The link between the Jamaat and the state once again became weak and was close to breaking point but the Jamaat was able to resist the temptation of withdrawing from the electoral scene completely so that it avoided the fate of the Egyptian Muslim Brothers who had been similarly repressed by Nasser. It continued to function under cover of its social, educational and religious activities and thus stayed away from direct confrontation.[15]

But the greatest threat was also the one that was most insidious. The coup had indeed moved the political debate away from the ideological field towards issues of development. For Ayub Khan 'one of the major demands of independence was the elevation of national character, progress of the country and prosperity of the masses'.[16] He, therefore, undertook a massive programme of modernization and the institutional reorganization of the state and the economy. The government displayed a firm will to reform, modernize and above all depoliticize Islam. Two important institutions were set up to achieve this. These were the Institute for Islamic Culture in Lahore, and the Institute for Islamic Research in Karachi. Both were entrusted with formulating, developing and spreading a modernistic synthesis of Islam. Two particularly important steps were taken: the reform of Muslim family law so that polygamy was restricted, the procedures for divorce were regulated and the provisions concerning the protection of women were improved; and the appropriation by the government of the main religious trusts, often associated with traditional land-owning interests.[17] Finally, under the terms of the new constitution promulgated in 1962, Pakistan became the 'Republic of Pakistan' (from being the 'Islamic Republic of Pakistan').[18]

To religious parties it seemed as if the government was trying to methodically sap their bases particularly that of the most influential among them, the Jamaat-i-Islami. The Jamaat attacked the government on its secular and pro-Western orientations, as well as the lifestyle it promoted, particularly its deliberate disregard of the Islamic mode of life. These arguments, however, carried little weight when compared with the economic factors which worked in Ayub's favour. The only way in which the Jamaat could attack the government was to demand respect for civil rights. Its opposition to the dictatorship, however, only led to the Jamaat being further entangled within the knots of its own contradictions. Although Western style democracy still remained hateful from the theoretical point of view, it constituted, nonetheless, the primary condition for the political survival of the Jamaat and defending it remained the only possible strategy it could adopt.

Its insistence on remaining cloistered solely within ideological considerations and its inability to take into account socio-economic factors also weakened the position of the Jamaat. Religious issues remained on the fringe, even at the height of the challenge to Ayub Khan's regime when it was confronted with a veritable urban uprising on account of rising social inequalities and on the matter of salaries and prices. The Jamaat was marginalized on its left by Zulfikar Ali Bhutto while the issue of regional autonomy raised by Sheikh Mujibur Rahman in East Pakistan placed regionalist parties at the forefront of the political scene. This situation threw the Jamaat into disarray and paralysed most of its action. The rise to power of regionalist and socialist forces left it with no choice but to support those in a position of power.

After the resignation of Ayub Khan the Jamaat decided to collaborate with Ayub's successor, Yahya Khan. Convinced of the need to save the country from breaking up and from socialism, it entered into a coalition with centrist and rightist parties. In 1968 it launched a vigorous campaign against socialism and called for the unity of the Muslim peoples. Its student branch, the IJT, became at this time a militant organization, even taking recourse to violence to counter leftist organizations on the campuses.

Its participation in the 1970 elections, called by Yahya Khan, however, proved to be disastrous. During the campaign it seemed to be ahead of the other political forces but the results revealed that it had, in fact, suffered big reversals. The Awami League of Sheikh Mujibur Rahman won an absolute majority while the Pakistan People's Party became the most important political force in West Pakistan. The Jamaat had lost on both fronts. As Ahmad Muntaz writes, 'for twenty years, the Jamaat had been calling for democratic elections on the assumption that given a free choice, the overwhelming majority of the people of Pakistan would vote for Islam. And now that a fair election had been held, their expectations were shattered.'[19]

THE JAMAAT-I-ISLAMI AND THE FALL OF THE BHUTTO GOVERNMENT

Under Bhutto (1971–3), the Jamaat proved equally incapable of taking advantage of the opportunities offered by the assaults of the new Prime Minister on traditional power structures. Though it contributed greatly to the fall of the Bhutto government, it could not encash Bhutto's decline to its advantage.

Bhutto had been elected in 1970 on the basis of a socialist programme promising to reduce the socio-economic disparities in Pakistan.[20] In fact, his populist policies had led to the participation of new social entities in the political debate. The disillusion which followed however, matched, the expectations. The economic policies of the new power centre, it soon became clear, were meant more to reinforce its own base than to promote a more equitable distribution of national wealth. Bhutto sought, particularly, to obtain the favours of the landed aristocracy instead of implementing the vast land reforms he had announced. The middle classes were the ones most affected by Bhutto's policy and they were, therefore, the ones who opposed his regime the most. The nationalization of private schools (except those frequented almost exclusively by the elite) led to a decline in the level of education. The middle classes were, moreover, the most affected by the inflation arising out of, on the one hand the economic policies, and on the other, the increase in the price of oil in the mid-1970s.[21]

The authoritarian style of the Prime Minister and doubts about his commitment towards democracy also lost him a number of sympathisers. Allowing no challenge to his authority, Bhutto dissolved the provincial assemblies (NWFP, Baluchistan) when he could not control them and set up a special paramilitary unit, the Federal Security Force, to intimidate and eliminate his opponents.[22]

The loss of East Pakistan, in 1971, became the cause of a grave crisis of identity and brought the ideological problem, namely the problem of the 'reason for the existence' of Pakistan, back to the centre of the political debate. The creation of Bangladesh was seen by the priestly class as resulting from the failure to apply Islamic principles in governance. The deposed dictator Yahya Khan was strongly condemned for his non-Islamic behaviour. Moreover, the growing economic resources of the Muslim Middle East led to a renewal of interest in the Islamic heritage of Pakistan. In fact, the utilization of religious symbols played a major role in the struggle for power.[23] When he saw that he was gradually losing his foothold, Bhutto tried to play the Islamic card, but having been a protégé of General Mirza and one of the most anti-religious lieutenants of Ayub Khan, he continued to be seen as anti-religious but even more as an opportunist. In fact, the Pakistan People's Party (PPP) was never able to gain real support among devout Pakistanis. His alleged non-Islamic conduct never ceased to be the subject of political debate. Consequently, he could not draw any benefit from the re-Islamization of the national policy described earlier. The middle class then began to turn towards religious parties.

The growing unpopularity of the Bhutto government and the climate of extreme politicization which followed could not but benefit the Jamaat which had been singularly weakened by its defeat in the 1970 legislative elections and, after 1971, by its collaboration with Yahya Khan during the war he lost in East Pakistan. When, in 1976, it began forcefully to demand the implementation of the Sharia, it found its membership increasing by around 1,50,000 new entrants.[24] Its influence grew notably in the army where the elevation of General Zia-ul-Haq to the post of Chief of Staff later accentuated this phenomenon.

The resurgence of the Jamaat, however, started from 1972, when it succeeded in forcing Bhutto not to recognize the new state of Bangladesh as long as the Pakistani prisoners of war had not been repatriated.[25] In September 1972, Mawdudi met Bhutto in Lahore. He convinced the Prime Minister of the need to evict leftist elements from the PPP and promised, in exchange, to support Bhutto's draft constitution. Not, however, before getting him to rename Pakistan as the 'Islamic Republic of Pakistan' and to have him stipulate in the constitution that the Prime Minister and the President had to be Muslims. For the first time in Pakistan, Islam became the state religion. During this same meeting Mawdudi also demanded from Bhutto that democracy be strictly complied with as the *sine qua non* of a harmonious relationship with the government.

From 1973, the Jamaat-i-Islami began systematically to oppose the government. An altercation between a member of the Islami Jamiat-i-Tulaba (IJT), the student branch of the party, and a member of the Ahmadi community at the Rabwa railway station in Punjab resulted in a new national anti-Ahmadi campaign. This time the Jamaat took the leadership of the movement fully upon its shoulders by organizing rallies, meetings, processions and street agitations throughout the country. The government gave in and through a constitutional amendment declared the Ahmadis to be non-Muslims.

The last episode in the struggle between the Jamaat-i-Islami and the government took place during the March 1977 elections. The politico-religious opposition against Bhutto had consolidated under the leadership of the Jamaat and a grand alliance of rightist parties had been formed. This was the Pakistan National Alliance (PNA) which demanded the implementation of the 'Nizam-e-Mustafa' (the system of the Prophet). The Islami Jamiat-i-Tulaba had earlier won the university elections of 1976 and thus demonstrated that it constituted an important force within the university. Consequently, when the PNA launched its campaign for the inception of the 'Nizam-e-Mustafa' the IJT was able to mobilize the resources of the educational institutions against Bhutto. It, thus, played an important role in mobilizing students and in organizing political agitations through strikes and other types of demonstrations.

The 1977 victory of the PPP was due only to the manipulation of the elections and Bhutto's denials simply inflamed the opposition further. With the rise in civil disobedience, the main leaders of the PNA were arrested. The confrontation with religious parties slowly converted the demand for civil and democratic rights into a social, Islamic movement.

Bhutto contacted Mawdudi once again in an effort to end the stalemate but their meeting this time, on 16 April 1977 in Lahore, was fruitless. Bhutto then tried to counter the demand for the 'Nizam-e-Mustafa' by banning casinos and night clubs but this feeble attempt at re-Islamization was again criticized as being guided by opportunism and was rejected by the religious parties. Unable to put an end to the agitation by the PNA, the authorities were tempted to take recourse to more repressive measures and they tried to arrest Mawdudi. The PNA let in be known in no uncertain terms that the arrest of the latter would lead to rebellion by his sympathizers. Mediation by Saudi Arabia, however, enabled the deadlock to be broken.

At the end of his tether, the Prime Minister tried to rally the Pakistanis together under a nationalist and anti-imperialist programme, accusing the PNA and more particularly the Jamaat, of being supported by Americans. But on 5 July 1977, Bhutto was overthrown by a military coup and General Zia-ul-Haq took over.

THE ZIA PERIOD: FROM 'ISLAM AND DEMOCRACY' TO 'ISLAM OR DEMOCRACY'

It would be appropriate at this stage to cast a glance at the troubled relations prevailing between the Jamaat-i-Islami and General Zia-ul-Haq. The years during which the dictator presided over the fate of the country did, indeed, constitute a crucial period in the political history of the Mawdudist party. For the first and only time in its history, it was a part of the authority in power. In the perception of the world, its participation in government, though ephemeral, indelibly associated the Jamaat with military dictatorship. Conversely, this participation contributed not a little towards conferring on Zia-ul-Haq's regime the image of a fundamentalist power. This image continued to haunt the Pakistani dictator long after his death and it often serves even today (in a perfectly contradictory manner) as a referent in the analysis of Pakistan's foreign policy. Actually, a close study of the facts brings out a complex relationship, marked by reciprocal attempts at using each other as instruments, in which the real ideologies of the two contributed not a little to their being distanced from each other. The cooperation between the Jamaat and the military regime which, in the long run, was detrimental to the basic political interests of the former, was to prove to be a total failure.

The relations between Zia and the Jamaat were marked by ambiguity right from the start. To justify his coup and to widen his political base, Zia-ul-Haq appropriated to himself the demand for the 'Nizam-e-Mustafa' which had been the rallying point of the PNA during the electoral campaign. He thus hoped to restore the authority of the state and to take control of Islamic parties by including them within the regime and by making of their demands the ideology of the state. In his first speech to the nation he asserted, 'I must say that the spirit of Islam, demonstrated during the recent [PNA] movement, was commendable. It proves that Pakistan, which was created in the name of Islam, will continue to survive only if it sticks to Islam. That is why I consider the introduction of an Islamic system as an essential prerequisite for the country.'[26]

For the Jamaat, the decision to support the military regime was not an easy one. It disapproved of the coup and after having launched a campaign for Islam with democracy, it found itself in the position of having to choose between Islam and democracy. Though he had promised to erect an Islamic political and socio-economic order in the country, there was no denying that Zia was anything but democratic. Not without some cynicism Zia-ul-Haq claimed that his coup in fact preserved democratic rights as Bhutto, according to him, had no intention of complying with the agreement he had concluded with the opposition for organizing new elections; hence he had saved the country from being dragged into a bloodbath.

The Jamaat, for its part, hoped to head a coalition government and put pressure on Zia to organize elections. It was on promises of Islamization and restoration of democracy through the fresh polls that the Jamaat finally rallied round the regime. The Amir, Mian Tufail[27] chose, for his part, to concentrate exclusively on the implementation of the Sharia. For Mawdudi, the important thing was that power should be in the hands of pious persons and Zia-ul-Haq met this criterion. On 21 August 1978, an agreement was concluded between Zia and the Pakistan National Alliance for the formation of a government. The Jamaat-i-Islami was given the ministries of Production and Industry, Information, Oil and Minerals, Water and Electricity and Planning. The last was allocated to Ahmad Kurshid, the number two man in the party. For the first time in their history, it appeared to Islamic parties that they could not only work in a favourable environment but also enjoy state patronage.

On 21 June 1979, however, a month after Bhutto's execution, this government was dissolved. Officially, the members of the Jamaat resigned because of the perpetual postponement of the general elections scheduled initially for November 1979. From this date the Jamaat no longer refrained from criticizing the government for its tardiness in the process of Islamization but refused, to begin with, to rejoin the Movement for the Restoration of Democracy (MRD). It avoided, moreover, opposing Zia-ul-Haq too directly with whom it had collaborated in the Afghan conflict.[28]

Zia also began to distance himself from the Jamaat. This change of attitude could be seen in various measures the government took and which revealed the growing rivalry between the regime and the Mawdudist organization.

The strength of the Jamaat, or at least its political visibility, depended largely on the activism of the Islami Jamiat-i-Tulaba. In 1984, the government decided to outlaw all student unions.

Since the IJT was the most powerful among them and it had won the university elections the earlier year, the Jamaat was directly affected. In addition to the loss of visibility that it brought, the ban directly affected its recruitment, the IJT being the breeding ground from which the party drew its future members and office bearers. The few attempts at resistance by the more active members of the IJT were crushed, sometimes with utmost savagery.

This turnaround was all the more distressing as the authorities in power had, till then, looked on the IJT in a relatively benign manner. Between 1977 and 1982, they had, it seems, encouraged its activities on campuses in order to counter the influence of the Peoples Students Federation, with leanings towards Bhutto.[29] After the latter's execution, however, those in power radically changed their strategy. The Afghan conflict and the support of the United States conferred on Zia-ul-Haq the international legitimacy that he had lacked. He also felt more confident on the home front where he found new allies among the apolitical *ulama*. He therefore felt less dependent on a Jamaat-i-Islami which was likely in the long run to undermine his authority.

From 1984, Zia-ul-Haq decided to systematically promote, in Karachi, the Mohajir Qaumi Movement (MQM). Karachi had traditionally been a bastion of the Jamaat. It had won the municipal elections there with a wide margin and had installed one of its own people in the post of Mayor when, in 1986, Zia-ul-Haq decided to get rid of the elected municipality for the benefit of the MQM. The government had earlier dissolved several workers unions in state enterprises where the National Labour Federation, controlled by the Jamaat, had won the union elections. The Jamaat was banned from undertaking any activity within the three largest employing units of the public sector, the Pakistan International Airlines, Pakistan Railways and Pakistan Steel Mills. These two decisions constituted a serious setback to the party and had a permanent effect on its influence in Sind.

Despite the reciprocal relationship between Zia-ul-Haq and the Jamaat-i-Islami between 1977 and 1988, with each using the other as an instrument for furthering its own policy, and despite their contradictory interests and their respective strategies, their conflict is a pointer to the gulf and even opposition between their ideologies. It is, however, necessary to return for a moment to the policies of Islamization actually followed by Zia-ul-Haq.

Zia did, indeed, begin by trying to transform the socio-economic and political structure of the country in keeping with the principles of Islam. He thus reconstituted 'the Council for Islamic Ideology', a consultative body which had been set up for the sole purpose of giving advice on the measures to be taken to introduce a more Islamic system of government.[30] He also introduced, in December 1978, a system of Sharia courts entrusted with ensuring that the existing laws were in conformity with Islam. In 1980, a 'Sharia Federal Court' was set up. Very soon, however, he began to place his own ideology above that of the Sharia. In spite of the revival of the Council for Islamic Ideology, he exempted the decrees of martial law, as well as the tax system and the overall banking system from conformity with the Sharia,[31] declaring, moreover, that the decisions of the 'Sharia Courts' could not by themselves eliminate, nor even change an existing law. The provisions regarding the competence of the Sharia Federal Court were changed twenty-eight times between 1980 and 1985.[32] It is also significant, that the eight judges that comprised the Court were directly appointed by the President.

For the Jamaat, a Muslim society would not come into being simply because a majority of its members were Muslims. It believed that only an Islamic state, which worked towards the systematic Islamization of all fields of public or private life could bring it about.[33] The President of Pakistan saw things from a completely different perspective. Whatever his personal degree of devotion, Zia-ul-Haq always had a traditional view of the relation between politics and religion.

The state could not have and never had any objective other than to create an environment favourable to the harmonious working of the community of believers, without claiming to be itself a sacred entity. His policy of Islamization, therefore, did not seek any change in the nature of the state. While the legislation had to draw its inspiration from the Sharia it was, nevertheless, by itself autonomous. Problems with the state could only arise if it was opposed to the management of civil society by the Sharia. This was what, in hindsight, he reproached Bhutto with, in order to legitimize his own coup, but from the point of view of the Pakistani President the state and religion were truly exclusive of each other. Despite appearances, the attitude of the dictator was, from this point of view, infinitely closer to that of Jinnah than to the fundamentalists. The conflict between Zia-ul-Haq and the Jamaat-i-Islami was, in the final analysis, only another episode in the debate between the Muslim national homeland and the Islamic state.

THE JAMAAT ON THE TOUCHSTONE OF DEMOCRACY: AN IMPOSSIBLE SYNTHESIS

Over the years, tension had grown between the Jamaat and the regime, the latter making superb use of the principle of 'divide and rule' by pitting, from 1985, the Muslim League and other religious parties against the Jamaat. Consequently, in June 1988, two months before the plane mishap which took the Pakistani dictator's life, the new Amir, Qazi Hussein Ahmad launched a vast movement of protest against the government and announced that the Jamaat had entered into an agreement with Benazir Bhutto's PPP to bring down the regime.[34] The Jamaat could not ignore the fact that it had fallen into the trap of the policy of Islamization adopted by the regime.[35] It had distanced itself from the latter too late to check the loss of popularity that had begun during this period and which become only too apparent in 1985, at the time of the legislative elections, which the dictator finally decided to allow.

Its alliance with the PPP could not but be circumstantial. Being the dominant party within the alliance, the PPP decided to dissolve the Movement for the Restoration of Democracy (MRD). The Jamaat soon realized that its salvation lay only in an alliance with Islamic and right of centre parties and the Islami Jumhuri Ittihad (IJI) was set up at the instigation of the Inter Service Intelligence (ISI),[36] whose most important component was the Muslim League.[37] The results of this alliance were unexpected as the Jamaat obtained eight seats in the National Assembly and thirteen in the provincial assemblies.

The PPP won the elections all the same, even though with a small majority. Neither the IJI nor the PPP could cobble together a stable majority. In the game of intrigues that followed, the Jamaat found itself more and more marginalized. It then began to realize the extent of its dependence on the larger parties, in this case on the Muslim League. It became more acutely aware of the fact that it could only hope to influence national policy if it enjoyed a greater representation in Parliament, which again it could not do alone no more than it could by being within the IJI. For a while and in the absence of any other alternative, it was left with no choice but to adopt a policy of 'critical support', attacking the government incessantly but nevertheless supporting the government of Nawaz Sharif. When Nawaz Sharif entered into an alliance with the MQM in Karachi, taking the path that Zia-ul-Haq had followed before him and which had been one of the reasons for his antagonism with the Jamaat, the party had no choice but to break away from him.

It did this, however, only on 6 March 1990 after protracted and difficult negotiations with the PPP. On 6 August, however, President Ghulam Ishaq Khan dismissed the government on grounds of corruption before dissolving, in October, the national and provincial assemblies and calling for new elections. As Benazir Bhutto's party had no likelihood of returning to power in the immediate future, the Jamaat rejoined the IJT.

This time round, it had better success in the elections. Although the number of candidates it put up was smaller than during the 1988 elections, the Jamaat won the same number of seats in the national parliament and a larger number in the provincial assemblies. It remained, nonetheless, marginalized within the IJI which showed greater interest in its alliance with the MQM. Consequently, it was increasingly tempted to adopt populist policies and to consider going it alone during the next elections, which it did in 1993 after the resignation of Nawaz Sharif and his government. Till then, however, it continued to oscillate between the IJI and the PPP.

These elections, at which the Jamaat presented itself alone for the first time under its own banner, resulted in failure. It kept only three of the eight seats it had obtained in 1993 and its influence was further reduced. Neither the number of its representatives nor the balance of power within Parliament allowed it to play a forceful supporting role. It found itself reduced, even more than in the past, to playing the role of an opponent and was thereafter tempted to turn back to the mob.

In the month of June 1996, the Jamaat-i-Islami organized a series of meetings and demonstrations against the draft budget presented by a Bhutto government caught in a bind between the International Monetary Fund which demanded that the fiscal deficit be reduced before it granted new loans[38] and a public opinion exasperated by the corruption and impotence of the government and the successive increases in indirect taxes as well as the various plans for restructuring which the requirements of the IMF forced on it. At the end of its tether, the police fired on the demonstrators, killing two persons. Nawaz Sharif's Muslim League Party (MLP) then took over and launched a nation-wide campaign against the government. The Jamaat went a step further by setting up the 'Save Pakistan Movement' whose main objective was to fight against corruption.[39]

These events could have been just one more episode in the life of a country in which democracy still lay uneasy and where, therefore, agitation was an almost normal component of the political debate, with dramatization and theatrics constituting the customary weapons of the opposition. The crisis seemed, however, sufficiently serious to spur the President of the Republic, Farooq Leghari, the Chief Justice of the Supreme Court, Sajjad Ali Shah and the chief of the army, General Jehangir Karmat, to launch a joint appeal to the government urging it to take measures to check corruption and enjoining it to rapidly improve its economic performance. This signalled the approach of a political crisis which was soon to take shape in the form of the removal of Benazir Bhutto from the office of Prime Minister.

The Jamaat, however, either did not know how to, or was not in a position to take advantage of a crisis which it had itself initiated, at least during its final phase. The decision to fight it alone by refusing any alliance with other opposition parties, even when they appeared to have objectives identical to its own, prevented it, from the outset, from hoping to play a major role in the crisis. Aware that the choice before it was once again between probable marginalization within the victorious alliance and certain defeat, the Jamaat preferred to keep away and called for a boycott of the elections. Absent thereafter from Parliament, and convinced that time would come to its rescue,[40] it pinned its hopes, as a last resort, on the erosion of Prime Minister Nawaz Sharif's Muslim League Party and on the corruption prevailing in the Pakistani political system.

THE JAMAAT-I-ISLAMI AND THE RETURN OF THE ARMY TO POWER

The return to power of the army illustrated once again the ambiguity of the Jamaat with regard to democracy. It is needless, here, to detail the circumstances which led to the coup by General Musharraf on 12 October 1999. It is more important, on the other hand, to examine the remarks made by Qazi

Hussein Ahmad three days later in Peshawar, to the members of his party. The Amir of the Jamaat expressed his happiness at the coup but at the same time demanded an end to the state of emergency and a return to democracy. Praising the army and, more specifically its chief, Pervez Musharraf, who 'had done an excellent job by dismissing the government of Nawaz Sharif', he demanded simultaneously 'an even handed accountability and the constitution of an independent Election Commission to conduct free and fair polls in the country'.[41] He reiterated his remarks on the twenty-first of the same month before the workers of the party, asserting that in the past 'martial law and military regimes had done nothing for the needful'.[42]

While it remained measured, the reaction of the Amir of the Jamaat was sharper when the new head of state made Kemalism his model of political development. Qazi Hussein did not hesitate to remind Pervez Musharraf that Pakistan's destiny lay in the Islamic revolution. He also made thinly veiled threats asserting that those who opposed his party 'should know that the JI workers [were] ready to sacrifice their lives for the cause of Almighty Allah and His Prophet'.[43] The reaction of the provincial government was not long in coming. Qazi Hussein was banned from staying in the North-Western Frontier Province for thirty days.

With the passage of time the party insists increasingly on the return to democracy, denouncing, what is more, the inclusion of members of the earlier government within the new team and drawing the attention of the public to the fact that while the Jamaat had been 'quite vocal and determined in its resolve to oust Nawaz but the thing had not happened in the way it was expected'.[44]

As it happens, its position is hardly any different from that of a large majority of Pakistanis who are relieved at the departure of Nawaz Sharif but expect nothing from the army other than the restoration of institutions. This position is, for all that, not devoid of ulterior motives. By denouncing the military dictatorship as well as the MLP and the PPP, the two latter being presented as jointly responsible for the inevitability of General Musharraf's coup, the Jamaat claims once again to be a force to which recourse can be taken. However, even while it goes along with public opinion without ever being able to mould and structuring it around itself, it continues to take refuge in its role of an eternal opponent, pursuing its tireless and vain quest for power at the cost of a constant loss of ideological substance.

AN AMBIVALENT POLITICAL RECORD

After more than fifty years of political activism, the record of the Jamaat-i-Islami appears, to say the least, ambivalent. While it has succeeded in erecting a strong and solidly structured organization and has rapidly made its presence felt as an interlocutor in the face of successive power centres in Pakistan, it has not succeeded in establishing and developing its electoral base. While it often acts as a pointer to the political crises which periodically hit Pakistan and sometimes, by way of its ability to mobilize opinion, as their catalyst, it remains essentially a party playing a supporting role and has never been the main beneficiary of its own activism.

Several factors can be cited to explain this situation. The Jamaat, both from the point of view of its political discourse as also from that of the organizational consolidation of the party, has evolved the way it has as a result, largely, of its interactions with different Pakistani governments *vis-à-vis* which it slowly established itself as a partner to be reckoned with. After Partition, three distinct but connected processes contributed towards determining the nature of its political activism. The first was that it had to limit its sphere of activity to the Pakistani nation state; then it had to legitimize the notion of a Pakistani state and finally, because of the increased pragmatism by its leaders, it had often to compromise somewhat its ideology. These same factors also contributed, in no small measure, to reducing its influence. Its function of legitimizing Pakistan is getting eroded with the gradual development of a still uncertain but real Pakistani national identity, while the pragmatism of its leaders blurs and sometimes even contradicts its discourse, which reduces all the more its credibility. Finally, from the time of the Soviet invasion of Afghanistan, it is precisely the extension of the action of the Jamaat to areas which overstep the borders of the Pakistani nation state which has given it a means of influence within the state apparatus.

But while the poor political performance of the Jamaat arises out of the ideology of the party, as well as its sociology and its strategy, it also owes a great deal to the very evolution of Pakistani society. With the gradual assertion of a Pakistani identity by its citizens, the debate on the justification for the existence of Pakistan is losing its relevance. The essentially ideological discourse of the Jamaat is losing its appeal, with the political debate moving towards the ability of the state to respond to the economic expectations of its constituents. In fact, the ambiguouity of its approach towards democracy, its elitist nature and its reluctance to indulge in populist policies, its inability to satisfy the material expectations of its fellow citizens, the evolution of Pakistani society itself, have all combined to confine the Jamaat within the role of an eternal opponent.

THE JAMAAT AND THE ECONOMY

The economy has very definitely played a major role in the poor electoral results of the Jamaat. For the Jamaat, preoccupation with the economy has meant that it could not exclude any aspect of social life from the field of religion even while it wanted to project a modernist image and to remain in step with the times. As Olivier Roy has noted, 'the economic act (buying, selling, possessing, . . .) is just one aspect among others of human activity in general, governed as such by the Sharia'.[45] The definition of an Islamic economy proceeds, therefore, from an effort 'at systemization and conceptualization of the basic prescriptions laid down by the Sharia to construct a coherent whole capable of being implemented and [to offer] a third path between the two systems of the 20th century'.[46]

In the matter of economics, as indeed on every other subject, the Jamaat stands for opposition. Its foremost purpose is to distance itself from what it considers as the excesses of Western capitalism and from Marxism. While doing this, it does not so much define the hypothetical content of a specifically Islamic economy as it attempts 'to Islamize' the economy. The concept that Mawdudi outlined,[47] and with which his successors have remained content, explaining and interpreting it at length rather than developing it,[48] is that of a liberal economy tempered by moral constraints concerning the manner in which wealth should be acquired and spent.

Mawdudi believed in a capitalist economy based on the principle of free enterprise and competition. Private ownership of the means of production, moderate profits resulting from productive investments, as also the laws of supply and demand were, from his point of view, the basic characteristics and necessary mechanisms of an Islamic economic system.[49] 'Islam recognizes all the natural principles of the economic aspects of existence which have always formed the foundations of human economy and it only abolishes the bad principles, not by depending on the coercive power of the state but through the maximum amount of moral instruction and a small measure of external force.'[50] As long as wealth is earned by legal means, the state has no right to interfere with or deprive individuals of the right to private property. The negative aspects of capitalism lie in its excesses alone, which must be done away with in its own interest, so as to restore the healthy and normal process of competition and of acquisition of wealth in accordance with natural means. Contrary to the claims of the socialists, there is no need to effect a fundamental change in the relations of production to achieve a just and equitable distribution of wealth. Ownership of the goods of production by some individuals, to the exclusion of others, appears to Mawdudi to be the result of 'natural causes' which govern life and which impose disparities in the economic sphere. Salaried work and capital are, consequently, some of the traits characteristic of society and the inevitable consequence of complex economies.[51]

Exploitation and social injustice are the undesirable secondary effects arising out of the neglect of the needs of other members of the community. They are, therefore, the result of non-Islamic behaviour, characteristic notably of Western societies and leading to the division of society into classes permanently in conflict. In fact, in economics as elsewhere, Mawdudi explains once again the positive or negative character of policies as being dependent upon the ethical qualities of those who control operations. Everything rests, in fact, solely on individual virtue. In the vein of what the Muslim Brothers and the Iranian Islamists did later, Mawdudi condemns income which is not justified by work or by a risk that has been taken, but contrary to them, he seeks in no way to interpret Koranic prescriptions as a system authorizing the state to organize the redistribution of wealth.

Two issues dominate the debates on 'Islamic economy'. These are the *zakat*, which takes one back to the matter of social justice, and interest rates. The former is more a reminder of the obligation to come to the help of the needy than a truly economic problem. The second is, on the other hand, more basic because theoretically it involves the very working of the economy. In actual fact, however, it is once again the reflection of a basically moral issue. The prohibition on collecting interest on money that has been lent is indeed nothing but the prohibition on usury, and indirectly, on speculation. It is, on the other hand, permissible and normal to invest directly, or by contributing to the capital of another company, in productive activities and to derive profit from them or to share their losses, as the case may be. This is what Olivier Roy calls the 'conservative and technocratic version of Islamic economy'.[52]

The Jamaat's conception of Islamic economy is, therefore, at best, that of an economy having a moral base and focussed on the individual. It is hardly any different from the traditional Muslim concept of the economy[53] (nor even significantly so from the social-democrat stand on the matter). It simply lays down a certain number of conditions regarding the acquisition of wealth, making a distinction between the *halal* (legal) and the *haram* (illegal) from the Islamic point of view. These conditions relate basically to the degree of morality of the means by which income is acquired. Thus, drawing material benefit from trade in products or activities considered as immoral, such as trade in wines and alcoholic beverages, music, dance, corruption, theft, speculation, etc., is 'illegal'. It is also prohibited to use the wealth acquired by indulging in these same activities or products. God being the owner of all things and wealth being consequently only a gift of God, man must behave as if he is simply its guardian and use it in keeping with the prescriptions of religion.[54] The 'Islamization' of the economy is in fact largely, if not exclusively, rhetorical. It is, to borrow a comparison made by Olivier Roy, 'an interface between two systems: the one ethical and judicial (the Sharia), the other being the reality of universal economics'.[55]

The lack of success of the economic theses of the Jamaat is due, however, less to its content, which actually is very commonplace and relatively in keeping with the canons of orthodoxy of the time, than because it has been inadequately emphasized in the discourse and the programme of the party. Since it refuses to confer on the economy any supremacy in the scale of social values, the Jamaat has never been able to really highlight it, drowning the few elements of its programme in an excessively moralizing discourse in which corruption is the source of all the ills of the country and in which virtue is postulated as constituting the only surety of a healthy and effective management.

The period which preceded the dismissal of Benazir Bhutto and the holding of mid-term legislative elections in February 1997 provides a typical example of this phenomenon. The voting of the state budget which, under the pressure of international financial institutions once again reduced social welfare subsidies and increased indirect taxes, had served as the rallying point of an immense campaign of agitation throughout the country. During its entire duration however, Qazi Hussein Ahmad, while drawing the attention of the public to the calamitous state of the Pakistani economy, remained content with condemning 'the fascist, corrupt and un-Islamic government of the PPP'[56] without ever outlining the slightest programme likely to remedy the situation. In fact, the Jamaat had no solutions to offer for the concrete difficulties of its fellow citizens.

NOTES

1. Marc Gaborieau, 'Le néo-fondamentalisme au Pakistan: Maududi et la Jamaat-i-islami', in Olivier Carre and Paul Dumont, *Radicalismes islamiques*, Paris: l' Harmattan, 1986, p. 40.
2. Quoted in Sayyed Vali Reza Nasr, *The Vanguard of Islamic Revolution*, London and New York: I.B. Tauris Publishers, 1994, p. 106.
3. This same logic also led Mawdudi to give priority to the matter of education.
4. The issue of Jamaat and nationhood will be discussed later.
5. Sayyed Vali Reza Nasr, op. cit., p. 106.
6. Rafiuddin Ahmed, 'Redefining Muslim Identity in South Asia: The Transformation of the Jamaat-i-Islami', in Martin E. Marty and Scott R. Appleby (eds.), *Accounting for Fundamentalisms*, Chicago and London: University of Chicago Press, 1984, pp. 609–705, specially p. 670.
7. Sayyed Vali Reza Nasr, op. cit., p. 120.
8. Ibid., p. 121. This incident was not forgotten. When violence broke out again in 1989 in the Kashmir 'Valley', the Jamaat led the campaign for '*Jehad* in Kashmir'.
9. In fact, till 1977 the statutes of the Jamaat forbade its members from joining government service or the army and from holding elective offices. Marc Gaborieau, op. cit., p. 60.

10. Sayyed Vali Reza Nasr, op. cit., p. 122.
11. Ahmad Mumtaz, 'Islamic Fundamentalism in South Asia: the Jamaat-i-Islami and the Tablighi Jamaat of South Asia', in Martin E. Marty and Scott R. Appleby, *Fundamentalisms Observed*, London and Chicago: University of Chicago Press, 1991, pp. 457–530, specially p. 470.
12. The issue of the identity of Pakistan remained, nonetheless, at the centre of the political debate in Pakistan for some time still, as is dramatically demonstrated by the anti-Ahmadi controversy. The question of the status of religious minorities had been, for some time, a major problem because it highlighted the debate between Pakistan as the national homeland of Muslims and Pakistan as an Islamic state. In 1953 an orthodox religious party, the Majlis-i-Ahrar, demanded that the Ahmadis, considered as heretics by most Muslims on account of their rejection of the final nature of Mohammad's prophecy, be declared non-Muslims and that some Ahmadis occupying important posts, such as Chaudhury Zafarullah Khan, Foreign Minister of Pakistan, be dismissed from their positions. The disturbances which followed, linked also with the deterioration of the economic situation in Punjab (the Majlis-i-Ahrar linking the economic question with the Islamization of the state by underlining the presence of Ahmadi ministers in the government as well as the disparity between the wealth of the Ahmadi community and the poverty of the large majority of the Muslim population) led to numerous deaths and martial law was promulgated in Lahore. The Jamaat tried, in turn, to take advantage of popular discontent but entered into the agitation only with extreme reticence. The agitation, undoubtedly, opened up new opportunities, particularly the possibility of getting a more solid foothold in Punjab, but it presented, in tandem, a certain amount of risk. Mawdudi realized that participation in riots might sully the image of the party and that the question of the Ahmadis would be resolved once a genuine policy of Islamization had been undertaken. This was his argument against the agitation with the Ulamas. The activism of the Majlis-i-Ahrar and the reaction of the government, however, led the Majlis into disarray and forced it to choose camps, thus dragging the Jamaat into the agitation. On 5 March, Mawdudi published the most systematic denunciation of the Ahmadis, under the title *The Qadiyani Problem*. Meant essentially to restore its pre-eminence within reli-

gious circles, this publication turned Mawdudi into the main figure of the agitation even though he had always been opposed to it. He was accused by the government of inciting hatred among religious communities in Pakistan and of breach of martial law. He was arrested, put on trial and sentenced to death. His sentence was later commuted into life imprisonment and Mawdudi was set free in April 1955. This episode did not, however, erode the commitment of the Jamaat to the preservation of civil liberties. Wilder Andrew, 'Islam and Political Legitimacy in Pakistan', in Syed Muhammad Aslam (ed.), *Islam and Democracy in Pakistan*, Islamabad: National Institute of Historical and Cultural Research, 1995, pp. 31–88, specially p. 40. Sayyed Vali Reza Nasr, op. cit., p. 137.

13. Marc Gaborieau, op. cit., p. 61.
14. This contradiction will be discussed in detail later.
15. When in 1962 political activity was once again permitted it was the first to return to the forefront of the political scene with its strength almost intact. See Ahmad Mumtaz, op. cit., p. 472.
16. Quoted in Ahmad Mumtaz, ibid.
17. Ibid., p. 472.
18. A certain number of 'Islamic' provisions however remained unchanged.
19. Ahmad Mumtaz, op. cit., p. 476.
20. At the time of Ayub Khan's resignation the percentage of the poor, that is to say of persons with an income less than Rs 300 a month, had decreased. It had come down from 60.5 per cent to 59.7 per cent in the rural areas and from 54.8 per cent to 25 per cent in the urban areas. The disparity in incomes had, however, increased, both between the provinces as between the rich and the masses. In 1968 some 22 families controlled two-thirds of the industrial assets, 80 per cent of the banking industry and 70 per cent of the insurance sector in Pakistan. Corruption also had grown in considerable proportions. See Sayyed Vali Reza Nasr, op. cit., p. 163.
21. Andrew Wilder, op. cit., p. 53.
22. Ibid., p. 54.
23. Ibid., p. 53.
24. Sayyed Vali Reza Nasr, op. cit., p. 173.
25. Ahmad Mumtaz, op. cit., p. 477.
26. We will return later to this aspect of the relations between the Jamaat and Zia-ul-Haq.

27. He succeeded Mawdudi in 1973, when the latter having resigned for health reasons.
28. I will return later to this aspect of the relations between the Jamaat and Zia-ul-Haq.
29. During this period the IJT enjoyed on the campuses an almost total right of veto on admissions of students as well as recruitment and promotion of teachers in almost all the twenty universities of Pakistan. See Ahmad Mumtaz, op. cit., p. 483.
30. Three fields were particularly targeted by this institution: Islamic taxes (*zakat*) and agricultural taxes (*ushr*), interest rates and the Islamic penal code. See John L. Esposito, 'Islam: Ideology and Politics in Pakistan', in Ali Banuazizi and Myron Weiner, *The State, Religion and Ethnic Politics: Afghanistan, Iran and Pakistan*, Syracuse and New York: Syracuse University Press, 1986, pp. 320–70, specially p. 343.
31. John L. Esposito, op. cit., p. 343.
32. Charles Kennedy, 'Islamization under Zia', in Syed Muhammed Aslam, op. cit., pp. 135–46, specially p. 135.
33. See Frédéric Grare, *Le Pakistan face au conflit afghan (1979–85): au tournant de la guerre froide*, pp. 107–9.
34. Ahmad Mumtaz, op. cit., p. 484.
35. Which Mawdudi, nevertheless, supported till his death in 1979.
36. Hostile to the PPP, the ISI was generally interested in the continuation of Zia-ul-Haq's policy and more particularly in the continuation of the war in Afghanistan. See Sayyed Vali Reza Nasr, op. cit., p. 206.
37. It should be noted, however, that the Amir, Qazi Hussein Ahmad, was opposed to the participation of the Jamaat in the IJI and reconciled himself to it only in the absence of a counter-proposal from the PPP. The Jamaat faced the possibility of a severe defeat if it went into the elections alone. The Jamaat found itself again, however, in disarray, forced to explain to the public the reasons for its participation in a pro-Zia alliance when it had fiercely fought the latter earlier. It tried to get out by laying stress on its common stand with the armed forces in the management of the Afghan conflict. See Sayyed Vali Reza Nasr, op. cit., p. 207.
38. *The Economist*, 19 October 1996, p. 67.
39. *Pakistan Political Perspectives*, Vol. V, No. 10, October 1996, p. 79.
40. Qazi Hussein Ahmad, the Amir of the Jamaat, declared to the author that his party would come into power within five years.

41. *Pakistan Political Perspectives*, Vol. VIII, 11 November 1999, p. 44.
42. Ibid., p. 45.
43. Ibid.
44. *Pakistan Political Perspectives*, Vol. VIII, 12 December 1999, p. 52.
45. Olivier Roy, *L'échec de l'Islam politique*, Paris: Le Seuil, 1992, p. 167.
46. Ibid., p. 169.
47. Sayyed Abul Ala Mawdudi, *The Economic Problem of Man and its Solution*, Delhi: Markazi Maktaba Islami, 1989.
48. This last assertion needs, however, to be moderated. The Islamic Foundation of Leicester, in England, has recently concluded an agreement with the 'Loughborough University of Technology' to teach Islamic economy. The students attend courses for a little over a year for a 'Master of Science' degree which can, if required, lead on to a Ph.D. In addition to the 'conventional' teaching of economics, students are trained in the principles of Islamic economics and finance, a large part of which relates to 'the understanding and management of financial and monetary working without rates of interest', *to Study Islamic Economics and Finance at a British University*, Leicester, U.K.: Loughborough University of Technology, Department of Economics, in cooperation with the Islamic Foundation. The existence of a doctorate programme seems to indicate quite clearly a desire to move towards research. It should be noted, however, that this initiative has originated from an organization of the diaspora and not the 'parent' organization (if this word has any meaning in the case of the Jamaat networks).
49. Yousef M. Choueiri, *Islamic Fundamentalism*, London: Pinter Publishers, 1990, p. 116.
50. Sayyed Abul Ala Mawdudi, op. cit., p. 28.
51. Yousef M. Choueiri, op. cit., p. 116.
52. Olivier Roy, op. cit., p. 178.
53. See on this latter subject, Rodinson Maxime, *Islam and Capitalism*, Paris, Le Seuil, 1966.
54. See particularly Muhammad Muslehuddin, *Economics in Islam*, Lahore: Islamic Publications, 1994, p. 43.
55. Oliver Roy, op. cit., p. 183.
56. *Pakistan Political Perspectives*, Vol. V, No. 9, September 1996, p. 71.

4. Geostrategy of the Jamaat-i-Islami

Olivier Roy maintains that 'it is the strategy of the states and not the existence of a mythical Islamist international outfit which explains the place and the action of the Islamist movements'.[1] The Jamaat-i-Islami is not an exception to this rule and to speak of the geostrategy of the Jamaat-i-Islami comes down, by this very fact, to speaking basically of the Jamaat-i-Islami Pakistan. The Mawdudist organization undoubtedly enjoys a certain autonomy in the conduct of its operations. It also undoubtedly has a certain number of its own objectives, but its successes or its failures are primarily those of the state or of a part of the Pakistani state machinery as well as a sign of the relations it has developed with the latter.

THE JAMAAT-I-ISLAMI AND THE FOREIGN POLICY OF PAKISTAN

To explore the role of the Jamaat-i-Islami in formulating the foreign policy of Pakistan is to simultaneously examine the question of the Islamic nature of Pakistan's foreign policy, compare of the ideology of the Jamaat with the pursuit of the national interest of the Pakistani nation state as also the means available to the Jamaat for the pursuit of its own objectives. This means seeking simultaneously to investigate its ability to influence decision-making in the matter of foreign policy and to act in an independent manner so as to make its weight felt over the course of events in the direction dictated by the ideology of the party.

THE ISLAMIC NATURE OF PAKISTAN'S FOREIGN POLICY

To assert the Islamic nature of Pakistan's foreign policy presupposes not only that the eventual influence of Islam on one or another decision can be determined but that it can be systematically confronted, through the analysis of a certain number of concrete cases, with a referent in the form of an Islamic theory of international relations. This, however, hardly exists at present except in an embryonic state. The central concept is that of the *umma*, the community of believers, defined by the sole criterion of religious kinship. On account of the existence of Muslim communities living outside the 'territory of Islam', the *umma* oversteps and transcends the *Dar al-Islam*. It is basically a-territorial and, from a political perspective, it is necessarily 'unitary, messianic and universalizing'.[2] But this ideal, however desirable in the eyes of the believer, remains nonetheless distant or at least out of tune with contemporary reality. It consequently engenders a classification of states in accordance with their affiliation to the *Dar al-Islam* (abode of Islam) where the law of God is implemented, and the *Dar al-harb* (abode of war) where divine precepts are not followed and which must be subjugated, if necessary by war.[3]

Besides, like every other foreign policy, that of Pakistan is conditioned by geostrategic constraints, the way its internal situation evolves, the conjunction of international circumstances and the ideology proclaimed by the authorities in power. Under such conditions, to make a clear-cut statement on the Islamic nature of Pakistan's foreign policy would be like asserting the primacy of the ideological factor over all the others, that is to say asserting that the formulation of the foreign policy is subjected to the sole objective of strengthening the dissemination of the faith on earth, 'Islam being considered as the means and the aim, the starting point and the end objective of every policy'.[4] Now, in Pakistan, contrary to what prevails in Iran, Islam is not considered to be a militant ideology, inspiring a combative foreign policy, but simply constitutes, to borrow the expression used by Mohammed-Reza Djalili, an 'ideology of assertion and of management'.[5] If, as Leonard Binder affirms, 'official Islam is . . . closely identified with the state, its function, as of old, remains the maintenance and enhancement of social control'.[6]

The 'two nation theory' on which the creation of Pakistan was based and according to which there were in undivided India 'two antagonistic nations, motivated by diametrically opposed concepts, that of the Hindus and that of the Muslims',[7] could in no way be assimilated with any kind of Pan-Islamism. Contrary to the state of affairs which prevailed in Iran, until the war against Iraq, there is no disavowal in Pakistan of the nation-state or of nationalism. 'The idea of "nation" in the framework of a territorially demarcated state'[8] is not considered as foreign to Islam. Conversely, the state consolidates and legitimizes the idea of nationhood in opposition to ethnico-national ideology and gives it, while doing so, its coherence. All through the fifties and sixties indeed, the very existence of the state, dominated, it is true, by the Punjabis and the Mohajirs, was threatened by the claims to autonomy of the Sindhis, the Pashtuns and the Bengalis, which culminated in the secession of East Pakistan and a civil war in Baluchistan. Consequently, the government used religion as an element to deny all legitimacy to ethnicity by highlighting the transcendent unity of the community of believers. While on the one hand the ethnic factor continues to be relevant, it is nevertheless tending to tone down, and the cleavages in Pakistani society coincide less and less with regional administrative divisions which were fashioned in a precise manner underYahya Khan along ethnic lines of division. Islam continues, nonetheless, to play a role in the cementing of national unity.

This distinction takes us back to the concept which the founders of the nation had of the very idea of Pakistan, closer undoubtedly to the national homeland of the Muslims of the Indian subcontinent than to the Islamic state. This debate, which was the main line of cleavage between Jinnah and Mawdudi, remains topical to this day and divides 'secular' parties from Islamic parties. Till now, however, in spite of the concessions made by nearly all Pakistani leaders to religious parties, the concept that has prevailed has been, including during the Zia-ul-Haq period, closer to that of a secular state than to that of a theocracy.

The influence of Islam on the foreign policy of Pakistan does not in any way call into question international norms, or the organization of states into a hierarchy. In the matter of international relations, Jinnah never drew from his 'two-nation theory' anything other than a most conventional concept of foreign policy, asserting notably that 'we wish to live in peace and harmony with our neighbours as a free and independent people. We wish our people to develop to the fullest of our spiritual, cultural, economic, social and political life in a way that we think best and in consonance with our own ideal and according to the genius of our people.'[9] This in no way prevented a more marked sympathy for a certain number of Muslim countries, the foremost of these being Saudi Arabia. There does exist, it is true, an important current of Pakistani foreign policy sometimes called the 'Muslim school', which would like to see a greater weight being given to the ideological factor and which is inclined to promote the establishment of a strategic consensus between Muslim states in order to counterbalance American imperialism and the Judeo-Christian 'peril'. Pakistan is expected to play a major role in the establishment of this consensus on account of its importance as a Muslim state.[10] The supporters of this concept, among whom can also be counted the Jamaat-i-Islami, are however in disagreement over a number of issues. While some see in the establishment of the above-mentioned 'strategic consensus' an essentially political alliance, others see its significance in military terms. They have, moreover, divergent views with regard to the choice between Iran or Saudi Arabia as their main partner. It should, perhaps, be noted that this school represents just one current among many others,[11] and that none of these different trends is specific to an institution, personality or regime. One can very often perceive the (partially) contradictory influences of each of these currents in the way they approach the same problem, their sole common denominator being their anti-Indian character. The highly personalized and centralized nature of Pakistan's foreign policy, moreover, makes for great fluctuations, according to one or another school being predominant, in accordance with the circumstances of the time. It would, hence, be unfair to call Pakistan's foreign policy Islamic.[12]

Does this mean that the Islamic factor has no relevance whatsoever? Obviously not. Islam is cited in a number of causes defended by the Pakistani state. Pakistan's handling of the Afghan conflict was based on this approach. Zia-ul-Haq was criticized in his time for having given explicit support to the Islamist groups in the Afghan resistance. This policy was, however, less due to ideological considerations than to a desire to strengthen the security of the 'land of the pure'.[13] In the face of the militant atheism of the Russians, it was important to give the resistance a religious colour. Islam provided a common link and could become a powerful mobilizing force. Once the Soviet invader had left, Pakistan again used the Islamic card to try and transcend Afghan ethnic divisions and thus gain access to the routes to Central Asia.

Even in Kashmir where, in consonance with the logic of partition, the presence of a Muslim majority population within the former princely state became the basis of Pakistan's claim for its unification with the 'land of the pure', a similar phenomenon can be observed. No matter which government is in power, Islamabad always supports the prominent Kashmiri parties fighting against the Indian 'occupier', irrespective of their ideology. It is only in recent times that it has begun to support Islamist groups such as the Jamaat-i-Islami for the sole reason that it is today the only one which advocates the unification of Kashmir with Pakistan. It is, moreover, striking to note that Pakistan has put forward its claim only against India although China controls more than 19 per cent of Kashmiri territory. This is due to the better relations between Beijing and Islamabad as well as to the realistic attitude of Pakistan's decision-makers. It demonstrates, however, once again, that the logic of national interest prevails over ideological considerations.

Generally speaking, whether it is the matter of Kashmir, Afghanistan or Central Asia, the Islamic factor is used to manage conflict and to rationalize Pakistani choices rather than as a determinant of its objectives. As Islam is a component of the very definition of the nation-state of Pakistan, it is an integral constituent of its foreign policy. Its importance varies in terms of the nature of the situation that the country faces at a given moment of its history. But that Pakistani irredentism in Kashmir is based on an Islamic rhetoric and that Islamabad pursues its objectives in the region by manipulating a certain number of militant Islamic groups, neither changes the nature of the problem nor the geographic extent of the claims. That this creates, in turn, certain difficulties for Pakistan, particularly on account of the risk it runs of a loss of control over these groups, does not change the nature of the Pakistani state.[14]

Since the Jamaat-i-Islami is not associated with the regime in power, the issue of its influence on Pakistan's foreign policy can be examined only in this specific framework, that is to say, in the partially or totally pin-pointed convergence of the geopolitical interests of the Pakistani nation-state and the ideological factor. It is, however, necessary, in order to truly measure its extent, to determine first of all its identity and to analyse the evolution of the position of the Jamaat-i-Islami on the issue of nationhood. Does it perceive itself as a Pakistani nationalist party or as a Pan-Islamist movement? A study of the theoretical and actual positions of the Jamaat uncovers a distinct difference between a discourse leaning towards universality and a practice which aims essentially (but not exclusively) at promoting the interest of Pakistan as a nation. This difference, it is true, arises partly out of the difficulty in formulating univocally what is the national interest. It reflects, in this sense, the extent of the possible interpretations of this term and takes one back to the central issue of the Pakistani identity.

The nationalist character of the Pakistani movement was to be forcefully demonstrated during the secession of East Pakistan in 1971. The Jamaat-i-Islami was the only party in what was to become Bangladesh which collaborated with the Islamabad government.[15]

THE JAMAAT-I-ISLAMI AND THE AMORPHOUS ISLAMIST INTERNATIONAL

It was on the basis of the central role of the first of three conflicts in which Pakistan was embroiled, the Afghan, the Kashmir and the Tajikistan, that the Jamaat-i-Islami acquired most of its capacity for action during the 1980s. The logistic capacities accumulated during this period enabled it to intervene to an appreciable extent, from 1989, in Kashmir, and then during the first half of the 1990s in Tajikistan. These same capacities enable it today to put training facilities at the disposal of the overall international Islamist orbit.[16] It is these actions, finally, which legitimize the doubts cast on the nature of the Jamaat-i-Islami (by itself or in relation to other movements ideologically akin to it) as threat to 'international security'.

To postulate the question of the terrorist nature of the Jamaat does not, however, imply that the answer is being prejudged.

It does not involve an inference on the existence of a specifically Islamist 'threat'. While they do fight for their cause, with weapons in hand, the Jamaat-i-Islami and 'like-minded parties' are not the only ones involved. The interests of the states of the region (Pakistan, naturally, but also India, Russia and the United States) also, directly or indirectly, enter into the definition and orientation of a 'threat'. It is not indulging in the fantasy of 'conspiratorial theories' to assert that the developments taking place in South and Central Asia are to a large extent the result of the manoeuvres of the secret services. But this does not mean that we should conclude that the Islamists in general and the Jamaat-i-Islami in particular are the docile instruments of one or another party. It is, on the contrary, their independence which is, to a certain extent, the reason for their importance and which makes it possible for them to be eventually manipulated.

The emergence of the Islamist orbit in Pakistan

The emergence, in Pakistan, of an Islamist orbit with an international character has been a gradual phenomenon. Islamism was, in fact, not an element imported into the country but was the result of a progression distinctive to the Islam of the subcontinent (or to some of its elements), with relation to its political evolution.[17] Very soon, however, bonds were established between representative currents of thought that became a source of anxiety to the Muslim world.

In the case of the Jamaat-i-Islami, intellectual influences and personal relations took precedence over institutional bonds.[18] Historically, the writings of Mawdudi are said to have been a source of inspiration to Hassan el Banna, the founder of the Muslim Brothers, and to Sayyed Qotb. Later, the Brothers played a significant role in the institutionalization of the Jamaat. Between 1952 and 1955, Said Ramazan, a Brother settled in Karachi, helped the Jamaat-i-Talaba, the main student branch of the Jamaat, to formalize its administrative structure. The bonds between the Egyptian movement and the Pakistani party were subsequently maintained and extended to other Islamist parties as and when they were set up.

Saudi Arabia played an important role in this process by providing the Jamaat the financial means to implement its objectives and, more than that, by gradually gathering the Islamist parties of the world under the banner of the Jamaat. It was in the early 1960s that the Jamaat began to forge ties with Saudi Arabia, when Mawdudi and Ahmed Kurshid both received the 'King Faysal' prize. This Saudi monarch soon became the main supplier of funds to the Jamaat, justifying his support to what he then perceived as the beginning of an Islamic Internationale, by, first, its stand against socialism, then against Shia fundamentalism. In the early 1970s the monarchies of the Gulf, troubled by the leftist leanings of Pakistan and taking full advantage of the oil boom, joined the Saudi monarch in his effort to prevent the advance of socialism and to destabilize Bhutto. Iran's Islamic revolution, followed by the Iran-Iraq war, marked a turning point, with each of the two countries trying to mobilize the Islamic parties of the world under their respective banners. In this struggle, which marked the beginning of the polarization of the Muslim world, the Jamaat sided with Saudi Arabia. It acquired, thereby, a position of privilege within Sunni Islamist organizations.[19]

It was, however, the Afghan conflict which was to make the Jamaat into a cardinal organization within the Islamist orbit. Well before the Soviet invasion, Afghanistan had marked out a field of action for the Jamaat-i-Islami Pakistan. The present Amir of the Pakistani Jamaat a Pathan by birth, who maintained excellent relations with the chief of the Afghan Hezb-i-Islami, Gulbuddin Hekmatyar, himself a Pushtun, kept up, right from 1965, the link between his movement and Afghan Islamists.[20] This initial relationship made the Jamaat into a player in the Pakistani management of the Afghan conflict. Indeed, a division of tasks took place between the Jamaat and the Pakistani army. While the latter dealt directly with moderate

Afghan parties, the Jamaat was entrusted with managing the relations with Islamist parties, recognizing only the alliance with the latter as being representative of the resistance.[21] The Pakistanis soon established the infrastructure required to ensure their training.[22]

This initial influx of Afghan refugees in Pakistan was the origin of a series of developments of considerable importance in the overall region. In the normal course of events the Afghan Mujahideen should have returned to Kabul and activist organizations created at the time of the war should have been dismantled. However, nothing of the sort happened. The existing infrastructure, that is to say the training camps remained such as they were and were even further developed in some regions like Azad Kashmir. The 'Afghans' then began to put in an appearance in most of the 'trouble spots' of the Muslim world.[23]

THE JAMAAT-I-ISLAMI AND THE 'TROUBLE SPOTS' OF THE MUSLIM WORLD

The involvement of the Jamaat-i-Islami in the conflicts of the Muslim world varies, naturally, in terms of their proximity to it and also, partially of their degree of relevance to the foreign policy of Pakistan since much of its means of action depends on whether it is being used as an instrument by the Pakistani army. This involvement varies, ranging from active military combat to simple political support. The different levels of commitment can be likened to numerous concentric circles emanating, from the subcontinent to the areas surrounding the Mediterranean, crossing through the CIS, and then gradually vanishing from the point of view of material support from the party, partially compensated for by a rhetoric which is inversely proportional to the means deployed. However, the specific action of the Jamaat-i-Islami becomes more difficult to identify as one moves away from its 'natural' zone of influence. Testifying more to Islamic solidarity than to a definite military advantage, it gets swallowed up within the 'brother party' directly involved in the given zone of operations. Traces of the Jamaat-i-Islami can be found in the conflicts in the former USSR, Tajikistan, Chechnya[24] and Nagorno-Karabakh.[25]

The Jamaat believes that all CIS regimes are still vassals of Moscow and should consequently be replaced by Islamic regimes in consonance with what it assumes is the aspiration of the Muslim majority population. Its leaders are simultaneously conscious of the fact that seventy years of communism have deeply affected the religious culture of these people who need, first of all, to be re-Islamized. With financial aid from Saudi Arabia, the Jamaat is trying to give to the Muslims of Central Asia the religious instruction that they lack, by exporting religious works such as Korans and sacred texts, as also the writings of Mawdudi, and by setting up schools entrusted with teaching basic religious conduct such as prayer. The Jamaat has also reached a number of agreements with the authorities of the concerned countries so that the most brilliant or the most motivated among them can go and continue their studies in the most reputed universities of the Muslim world.[26] A similar strategy is in place in Sinkiang.

The action of the Jamaat is not restricted, however, to proselytizing. The party is trying to give, directly or indirectly, an active support to 'kindred parties' when these are faced with armed opposition from the authorities. This support can very often be deployed only thanks to the connivance of the Islamist parties and the ISI, some of whom had counted on Central Asia breaking away from the CIS, leading to a disintegration of the Russian Federation itself and the recomposition of a new structure dominated by conservative Islamist regimes.[27]

Afghanistan

The two conflicts in which the Jamaat has been particularly involved, those of Afghanistan and Kashmir, have also demonstrated the limits of its action. They need therefore to be examined closely. The intimate links between the Jamaat-i-Islami and the ISI during the Afghanistan war have already been established. Relations with the Pakistani government deteriorated, however, in 1992, when General Hamid Gul had to give up his position as the head of the ISI. After Najibullah's fall, indeed, Islamabad decided to accept a settlement which went against the Mujahideen groups of Sayyaf and Gulbuddin Hekmatyar, which had been favoured by the Jamaat.

The disagreement between the Mujahideen, more specifically between Massoud and Hekmatyar, was not new. Dating to before the Soviet invasion of Afghanistan,[28] the antagonism between the two men was only exacerbated during the conflict, their personal animosity leading to differences over matters of strategy. While Massoud preferred to fight, Hekmatyar spared his forces with a view to taking control of Kabul at the appropriate moment. Once the Soviets left, the rivalry between the two warlords increased. Massoud captured the Afghan capital in 1992, while Gulbuddin Hekmatyar was forced to position himself at its threshold, in Tcharasyab. The Jamaat then tried to bring about a reconciliation between the two before once again asserting its support to Hekmatyar when it became apparent that the antagonism between them was irreconcilable.

A relatively new phenomenon appeared in the autumn of 1994 with the emergence of the Taliban. Coming from the traditionalist *madrassas*, initially without any political agenda, they were nevertheless able to restore order in some of the regions they controlled[29] by putting an end to the atrocities of the local petty warlords. Gaining the sympathy of the people without having, in fact, to fight much, they advanced without difficulty up to the doors of Kabul. Hekmatyar himself was marginalized shortly thereafter and forced to abandon his base at Tcharasyab, which was soon occupied by the Taliban. The latter proved, however, as incapable as the Islamist leader of capturing Kabul and found themselves once again subjected to the crossfire of warring parties. Massoud then succeeded in allying himself with the Uzbek troops of General Dostom as well as with the pro-Iranian Shia party, Hezb-i-Wahdat. There was a stalemate thereafter between this alliance and the Taliban, the latter occupying about 60 per cent of Afghan territory.

The Jamaat played a significant role in Afghanistan for the last time when the Afghan Jamaat-i-Islami concluded a power sharing agreement, on 26 May 1996, with the Hezb-i-Islami. On 26 June, Gulbuddin Hekmatyar became Prime Minister once again of the government in Kabul and entered the Afghan capital after having been received with full honours by his sworn enemy, Ahmed Shah Massoud in his own base. The Jamaat-i-Islami Pakistan, particularly its chief Qazi Hussein Ahmad, played, it seems, an important role in bringing about this agreement. It was, in fact, on the invitation of the Afghan President Rabbani[30] that he undertook the mission of mediation which was to lead to the reconciliation between the former enemies.[31]

The Jamaat acted in this negotiation in accordance with its specific interests as it considered Afghanistan to be the battlefield of Western interests.[32] Qazi Hussein Ahmad refused to help in establishing a secular regime in Afghanistan 'which would be a negation of the very reason why so many people had been killed over the years'[33] and whose shadow he saw emerging behind the Taliban. As regards the latter, the Jamaat chief felt they were being manipulated by foreign forces and refused to entertain the possibility of all of Afghanistan falling into their hands, although he did not exclude their eventual participation in the government of the country at some future date. He considered the renewal of the alliance between Rabbani and Hekmatyar as a first step towards a general reconciliation in Afghanistan. It is true that in his eyes the alliance did not constitute a major change on the military plane, but it could prove to be psychologically important. The 26 May 1996 agreement, which took concrete shape in end June with the entry of Gulbuddin Hekmatyar in Kabul, only gave rise, however, to an extreme polarisation of the situation in Afghanistan. This was followed by the fall of Jalalabad, followed shortly after by that of Kabul on 27 September 1996. After this last event, the Jamaat found itself totally marginalized in Afghanistan.

To understand the full impact of the victory of the Taliban on the Jamaat-i-Islami, it is necessary to view the Afghan conflict in its regional and global context. Like every conflict, the Afghan war had both intrinsic and extrinsic value. The struggle for power in Kabul was a wager by itself for the Afghan parties, but this conflict also crystalized wagers external to it but of greater importance to certain regional and even extra-regional powers. Local factors apart, the continuation of the war in Afghanistan was the result of the unresolved problem of Pushtunistan, of Pakistani ambitions in Central Asia and of the persistence of Indo-Pakistani rivalry, as also Russian preoccupations over Central Asia and the issue of the Caspian Sea. The American policy with regard to Iran also affected, directly and indirectly, the manner in which events unfolded in the zone.

For Pakistan, the turn that events took in Afghanistan involved merely a change of tactics in the pursuit of long established objectives. It was important, first of all, to put an end to Afghan irredentism on the matter of Pushtunistan. From 1947 till the Soviet invasion of Afghanistan, the Afghan government[34] constantly demanded the return of the Pushtun areas situated on the Pakistani side of the 'Mortimer-Durand' line. This had poisoned relations between the two countries and served, above all, as a justification for the reverse alliance between Kabul and Delhi which the Pakistani government was trying hard to checkmate. Undoubtedly, the Afghan 'peril' was by itself, politically and militarily, manageable by Islamabad, but it could take on a different dimension in the event of a renewed conflict with India as Pakistan would then have to fight on two fronts.

Islamabad wanted more than anything else to make Pakistan the major route to the Indian ocean by the countries of Central Asia. This would enable it to avail of the foreign exchange generated by the transit of Central Asian goods and to procure new markets for its own products, as also to improve its strategic position which had become considerably undermined since the Soviet withdrawal from Afghanistan (while, incidentally, benefiting from the American embargo on Iran).

These were the objectives that dictated the policies adopted by Pakistan during and after the Soviet invasion in Afghanistan. By relying mostly (but not exclusively) on Hekmatyar, the ISI, and with it the Pakistani government as a whole hoped, till the autumn of 1994, to be able to reconcile the demands of Pushtun nationalism with a pan-Islamism which would enable it to transcend Afghan ethnic divisions in order to ensure (directly or indirectly) its control over Afghanistan and to extend its reach towards Central Asia.

As far as Russia was concerned, the Afghan conflict legitimized and strengthened its policy in Central Asia. This fitted into the framework of Russia's general objectives with regard to the CIS defined by Boris Yeltsin[35] but it also fitted in with other, more specific objectives.[36] Fearing or pretending to believe[37] in the Islamist peril, the Russians perceived Central Asia as a first line of defence against a possible penetration by Iran, Pakistan and to a smaller extent, Saudi Arabia.[38] Consequently, the perpetuation of the civil war in Afghanistan was in pursuance of their policy of support for the creation of indigenous military forces, the deployment of Russian border troops in the most vulnerable countries[39] and the maintenance of their political influence in the region. It also prevented any attempt at an autonomous opening up of Central Asia from the south. Turkmenistan and Uzbekistan, which do not have any access to the sea and which try to export their raw material[40] through the Indian ocean, saw their development blocked by the continuation of hostilities.[41]

Under these conditions, the perpetuation of the conflict was a blessing for Moscow which could maintain its influence at little cost over the entire region. As this policy was not devoid of risk on account of the attempts at penetration by some

Islamist networks, Moscow did not remain content with taking passive advantage of the situation created by its withdrawal from Afghanistan. The Russian leaders exploited the differences between the two main Mujahideen chiefs, Massoud and Hekmatyar, to regain a foothold in Afghanistan by giving to the former the logistic support that he lacked.[42]

The reconciliation that took place in May 1996 between Rabbani/Massoud and Hekmatyar created at the same time a *de facto* alliance between the Russians and an overall Islamist camp which consisted of the Hezb-i-Islami of Hekmatyar,[43] the Jamiat-i-Islami of Rabani/Massoud, the Ittihad-i-Islami of Sayyaf and the pro-Iranian Hezb-i-Wahdat to which should be added the Uzbeks of General Dostom. This alliance which, with the exception of Dostom, had earlier fought against the Soviets in the name of faith, now found itself aligned with its former enemy, fighting against other Muslim groups, in this case the Taliban.

Pakistan, considered till then as one of the main supporters of the Islamists in the zone on account of the special bonds that existed between the Jamaat-i-Islami and the ISI, found itself caught in the trap of a Delhi, Moscow, Teheran triangle. However, though it had decided to support the Taliban[44] against the Islamist parties, it continued to be accused of being the main ally of the latter, partly on account of the confusion reigning in the media, in political circles and the general public, on the very nature of Islamism and on the singularly selective and fluctuating concept of the proper use of human rights. This played no small part in marginalizing it on the international scene even though Benazir Bhutto tried hard to present Pakistan as a 'front line country' in the struggle against terrorism and extremism[45] in order to renew economic ties with the United States as well as the strategic alliance which had governed the relationship between these two countries during the 1980s.

The configuration of the Afghan conflict before the fall of Kabul was partially in consonance with American objectives in the region since the opposition of the Taliban to the Shia and pro-Iranian Hezb-i-Wahdat constitutes a serious obstacle to Teheran's ambitions in Central Asia and reinforces the strategy pursued by the United States of isolating Iran, without having to conduct a really active policy in the zone. At the same time, it had serious consequences for the security of Western interests, particularly in the Persian Gulf. The same Islamists[46] who had so ably served the Western camp in its fight against the Soviet Union during the Afghanistan war, turned against it and now offered refuge to the elements which were attacking its interests.[47]

In these circumstances, the capture of Kabul by the Taliban was a major setback to the Jamaat-i-Islami and, to a lesser extent, to its 'allies'. Since the Hazaras were suddenly reduced to their initial state of being a fringe element, Iran saw its already limited influence in Afghanistan eliminated at one stroke. Massoud having been forced to retreat towards the northern border,[48] Russia feared less a destabilisation of Central Asia than a loss of influence in the region, since the Central Asian republics were in a position to take advantage, if necessary, of the possibility (though still limited) of an opening through Afghanistan.[49] India suddenly lost a not negligible means of pressure on Pakistan, which in a way broke the circle of which it had become a victim for some months. The strategic situation of Delhi was not, however, significantly affected.

The Jamaat-i-Islami, which till 1996 was one of the main factors in the Afghan policy of Pakistan, was more severely affected. President Rabbani was the first to flee while Commandant Massoud took refuge in Panjshir. Its main ally, the Hezb-i-Islami[50] of Gulbuddin Hekmatyar was in disarray. In fact, the Jamaat lost within a few days all its influence in Afghanistan and, consecutively its utility for the ISI. This was a biting setback for the Jamaat-i-Islami and dramatically affected its capacity to influence Pakistan's foreign policy. Massoud's resistance still gives it some margin for manoeuvre but this remains both narrow and precarious.

Kashmir

Marginalized on the Afghan scene, the Jamaat continued to play a major role in the Kashmir arena. The conflict in Kashmir, which has been the main obstacle to the normalization of relations between India and Pakistan, entered once again into an active phase in 1989. It has become for the Jamaat-i-Islami Pakistan a national cause.[51] The revolt was initially launched not by the Jamaat itself but by the Jammu and Kashmir Liberation Front (JKLF),[52] a secular organization fighting for the independence of a Kashmir reunified within its pre-1947 borders.[53] In early 1990, the JKLF organized a campaign of mass protest against Indian domination. From the end 1990, however, it became evident that the leadership of the revolt was slipping into the hands of the Hizbul Mujahideen, the armed branch of the Jamaat-i-Islami Jammu Kashmir,[54] which has close links with the Jamaat of Azad Kashmir and the Pakistani Jamaat.[55]

Pakistan gave most of its support to the Jamaat and to the organizations that it controlled, to the detriment of a JKLF considered to be too autonomous and which, moreover, supported independence and not unification with Pakistan.[56] From 1991 the Hizbul Mujahideen became the main armed force among the Kashmiri insurgents,[57] and has continued to be ever since.

After Partition, the leadership of the Jamaat had decided to set up two distinct units situated on either side of the ceasefire line. This initial decision determined their preliminary mode of functioning. While the Jamaat-i-Islami of Azad Kashmir operates essentially like a branch of the Pakistani Jamaat and receives its instructions from Lahore, the Jamaat-i-Islami of Jammu Kashmir presents itself as a totally independent movement both with regard to Pakistan[58] and to India. The Jamaat-i-Islami of Jammu Kashmir operates within a Muslim majority environment in a region where the struggle for independence is in line with tradition as Kashmir was an independent entity till the arrival of the Mughals.

Considering the situation which prevailed at the time of its creation, the Jamaat-i-Islami of Jammu Kashmir was not, surprisingly, a political party from the outset. During the first three decades of its existence it operated according to Muntaz Ahmad, as a revivalist movement. Although rejecting Indian sovereignty over the region, it did not participate in the political struggle as it was of the view that the effort at Islamization of Kashmir would necessarily lead to the advent of an Islamic state which would then join Pakistan. It, therefore, stuck to its demand for a plebiscite, in accordance with the United Nations resolutions of 1949, 1951 and 1957.

It was only after Iran's Islamic revolution in 1978 that the Jamaat changed its course to turn to political activism and came, eventually, to spearhead the struggle for the 'liberation of Kashmir'. In August 1980 the leader of the student wing of the Jamaat called publicly on Kashmiri youth to work for the advent of an 'Iranian type Islamic revolution in Kashmir in order to achieve independence from India'.[59] Since then, the refusal to accept Indian sovereignty over Kashmir constitutes the single-point political programme of the Jamaat.

With 2,000 members and some 1,00,000 sympathizers, the Jamaat-i-Islami of Jammu Kashmir demands, like the other political parties of the Kashmiri opposition, a referendum on self-determination, but, in consonance with the position of its Pakistani counterpart, it does so in accordance with the already mentioned United Nations resolutions. This point is an important one because these resolutions offer the Kashmiri population the choice only between joining India, that is to say maintaining the *status quo*, and joining Pakistan. The Jamaat and the organizations affiliated to it (Hizbul Mujahideen) are the only significant political bodies[60] which demand unification with Pakistan. In fact, their role within the Kashmiri opposition is a singularly ambiguous one.[61] The Jamaat-i-Islami of Jammu Kashmir functions, in fact, as an appendage of the Jamaat-i-Islami Pakistan with which it can be considered as analogous both on account of its demands (unification with

Pakistan) as well as on account of its ideology, particularly, that part of it associated with politics.

The strategy adopted by Pakistan in Kashmir consists of the propagation of religious fundamentalism in order to promote separatism; the training and indoctrination of leaders selected in the Valley to form groups of activists; the training of young people in acts of sabotage and attack on the security forces, in the use of automatic weapons and the handling of explosives; and the training of special teams of agitators to trigger incidents to tarnish the image of a democratic and secular India. These agitators then approach different organizations of activists. By increasing unrest in the region, they incite the Indian government to respond with brutality and thus try to convince international public opinion that Delhi is constantly engaged in the large scale violation of human rights in Kashmir.[62]

The Jamaat-i-Islami plays a central role in this strategy. It helps in the recruitment and training of foreign combatants for the Kashmir cause. The influx of foreign volunteers in the Valley started in 1991. It was made possible by the Afghan connections of the Jamaat and the mobilization of its international networks. To begin with, its role was limited and only a few members of the Afghan Hezb-i-Islami joined the ranks of the Hizbul Mujahideen where they played the role essentially of advisers.[63] Their numbers became really significant only in 1992 after the fall of the Najibullah regime. They were soon joined by the Sudanese, Egyptians, Arabs from the Gulf, Pakistanis and Palestinians.[64] In 1993, their number was said to be between 600 and 1,000 and is, reportedly, in the neighbourhood of 1,200 men today (out of the nearly 10,000 activists within the overall organizations operating in the Valley).[65]

The Jamaat contributes also by mobilizing international pubic opinion and collecting funds. The foreign organizations connected with the Jamaat in the subcontinent, as also in Europe and in the United States, contribute by popularizing the cause of Kashmir which returns in their columns like a sort of leit-motif. The same networks also collect funds meant, in all probability, to finance the Kashmiri guerilla warfare.[66]

The Jamaat-i-Islami is, finally, the main vector of the 'Islamization' of those opposed to the Indian presence in Kashmir. Young people recruited by it, often right in school by teachers who themselves belong to the party, or later from the University, are systematically indoctrinated in accordance with the methods described earlier.[67] But the Islamization of the resistance is conducted also on another level which needs to be specified. While the majority of the Kashmiri population is, indeed, Muslim, it is not 'Islamist'. Only a few rural pockets controlled by the Jamaat and whose real importance it is difficult to assess,[68] claim to be faithful to this ideology. The political representation of the resistance reflects this reality. Out of the twenty-seven parties that the All Party Hurriyat Conference (APHC) is made up of, only the Jamaat-i-Islami claims to be Islamist. Its military activity, however, confers on it a visibility greater than that of the other components of the APHC. It, thus, contributes towards projecting to the outside world the image of an Islamist resistance, which Indian propaganda exploits at every possible opportunity.

As mentioned already, the Jamaat-i-Islami is also the only significant Kashmiri party which advocates unification with Pakistan. In this respect it is in opposition to the majority of the people of Kashmir who only aspire to independence,[69] and the other parties of the APHC who also want independence. Its importance and the probability that it is through the Jamaat that the members of the anti-Indian coalition obtain from Pakistan the funds required for their action, explains both the fact that the Jamaat is still tolerated within the coalition[70] and that the only claim openly advanced by it is a referendum for self-determination, no party leader wishing to publicly admit his real aspirations. All admit in private, however, that they desire independence.[71]

By blurring the image of the resistance the Jamaat-i-Islami manages to serve the interests of both India and Pakistan. Over

Kashmir, the two countries are in agreement over one single point, their refusal of independence for the region. The Jamaat-i-Islami is in this respect, their best agent. The Indian forces are aware of this and have made the Jamaat and its various 'subsidiaries' the chosen target of their repression.[72] The Jamaat appears, consequently, as the only hero of the fight against the Indian 'occupier' but its activism is conducted for the benefit of Pakistan and not for the independence of Kashmir. The Jamaat serves, in a way, as a foil to the political opposition which helps to divide, weaken and alienate from the majority of the population. The election of 1996 showed that, the people, tired of being caught in the crossfire between the Indian army and the activists, were progressively losing all interest in the armed struggle and were gradually getting resigned to the idea of the maintenance of the *status quo*.

Worried at the erosion of its base, which threatened in the long run its very existence, and aware of Kashmiri opinion, the Jamaat-i-Islami Jammu Kashmir elected in 1997 a new Amir, Ghulam Mohammad Butt, in place of Maulana Hakim Ghulam Mohd. The hardliners, led by Syed Ali Gilani, who had till then been the firmest supporter of armed activism, were temporarily marginalized. On 23 October Ghulam Mohammad Butt declared, to everybody's surprise, that he wanted to seek a negotiated settlement. This hardly changed the state of things in Kashmir. In the absence of a real will both on the part of India and Pakistan to put an end to the conflict, and confusion over the goal to be achieved by Pakistan, the Jamaat-i-Islami Jammu Kashmir found itself in a position of having to wait and watch. Though this policy exposed personal rivalries and differences of opinion among the leadership with regard to the strategy to adopt, it also offered the Jamaat an honourable way out, whatever the outcome. If a negotiated settlement materialized, the party could claim credit for it. If the situation deteriorated, as happened during and after the events of spring 1999, the Jamaat could advance the most hawkish among its hardline elements. Not really having the means to influence the course of action it could go along with it, whatever happened, adapting to events, since it could not control them.

In the spring of 1999, when the Pakistani army infiltrated *en masse* into the Mujahideen, Qazi Hussein Ahmad met Syed Salahuddin, the chief of the Hizbul Mujahideen in Lahore, in the presence of the press. The operation conducted at Kargil by the Mujahideen had clearly been initiated by the Pakistani army but the Jamaat, very officially, supported the *Jehad* and did not fail to severely castigate the Nawaz Sharif government when, giving in to international pressure, it ordered the army to withdraw. Qazi Hussein, however, took care not to attack the army itself, which had instigated the operation and was therefore mainly responsible for the diplomatic fiasco.

In Srinagar the Jamaat-i-Islami Jammu Kashmir remained quiescent during the entire course of events, on account of a severe military crackdown. Things changed, however, after the conflict was over. The Hizbul Mujahideen launched once again its campaign of attacks against the Indian armed forces. At the same time, around a thousand young Kashmiris, disillusioned at New Delhi's inability to follow up the successes garnered by its policy of repression with any concrete political process and encouraged by the success of the Mujahideen whose withdrawal, following that of the Pakistani army, was more the result of American, and to some extent Chinese, pressures than any real success by the Indian army, made the transition to guerilla warfare. Gilani, and with him the most hawkish section of the Jamaat, returned thereafter to the forefront of a scene that it had never really left.

In the last episode of this saga, a group of the Hizbul Mujahideen led by Majid Dar proposed a ceasefire on 2 August 2000 to the Indian government on condition of an equivalent restraint on the part of the Indian army and the initiation, without prior conditions, of a dialogue with Pakistan as well as with the All Parties Hurriyat Conference (APHC), an alliance of the main factions opposed to the Indian policy in Kashmir. Whatever may have been the real role of the Jamaat in the decision of the Hizbul Mujahideen chief, it was intensely embarrassing to the Jamaat-i-Islami. Maulana Fazlur Rehman, the head of the Jamaat-Ulema ul Islam, the main supporter of the Afghan Taliban and a rival of the Jamaat-i-Islami, did not fail to seize the opportunity to further denigrate Qazi Hussein Ahmad. The announcement by the Hizb was made while the Amir of the Jamaat was in the United States. This strengthened the suspicion with regard to the Jamaat, in Islamist circles, which saw in the announcement proof of a collusion between the Pakistani government and the Jamaat on the one hand and between the latter and the State Department on the other. Qazi Hussein's party, then, had no alternative but to distance itself from the Hizbul Mujahideen and notably from its chief who was asked to go back on his offer. The proposal soon fell through, however, not due to any turnaround by the chief of the Hizbul Mujahideen but on account of contradictory trends both within the militant group as well as the Pakistani army. The existence of hardline as well as conciliatory factions both within the Jamaat as within its armed branch, led the Hizbul Mujahideen to hold on to its position without any significant change, in spite of proposals and counter-proposals by the Pakistani and Indian governments.

THE JAMAAT-I-ISLAMI AND THE PAKISTANI STATE: AN AMBIGUOUS RELATIONSHIP

In the light of the analysis so far, there is reason to examine more closely the relations between the Jamaat-i-Islami and the Pakistani state. Their relations seem to oscillate between each trying to exploit the other to achieve its ends and that of opposing each other. The Jamaat upholds the policy of the government every time Islamabad incites it to support one or the other Islamist movement anywhere in the world. (This was the case in Afghanistan and in Tajikistan, for instance. It was also the case during the Kargil conflict when some

Mujahideen were allowed to infiltrate into one of the posts overlooking Kargil in Indian territory, through the routes used by the Pakistani army.) Then the Pakistani state becomes the vector of the policy of the Jamaat, and vice versa. By supporting all action aimed at strengthening Pakistan on the international scene, the party of Qazi Hussein Ahmad increases its own internal margin of manoeuvre. It is in this spirit that the Jamaat supports the Pakistani nuclear programme (which in turn fuels its anti-Americanism each time the State Department puts pressure on Islamabad to put an end to this programme).

Conversely, the Jamaat's criterion for support or opposition to the authorities depends on whether the government support to the causes that are most ideologically important to the Jamaat in matters of external policy is whole hearted or half-hearted. Thus the alleged inadequacy of the support extended by Benazir Bhutto to the cause of Kashmir was a matter over which the Jamaat constantly criticized her. Nawaz Sharif, chief of the Pakistan Muslim League (PML), though closer to the Jamaat, often incurred its wrath during his first term in office, for the same reasons. It seems also that the government of Nawaz Sharif sometimes financed the activities of the Jamaat in Kashmir in order to turn its attention away from the national political scene. The Kargil operation, however, brought out openly the opposition of the Jamaat to Nawaz Sharif, whom it accused of having given in under American pressure.

This political opposition does not, however, mean that the position of the Jamaat is necessarily incompatible with the policy followed by Islamabad even on issues on which it is criticized by the Jamaat. Kashmir, once again, furnishes the best example. To safeguard its international image, no Pakistani decision maker wants to be seen as a troublemaker in the region, though he cannot even allow himself the luxury of abandoning the cause of Kashmir. Throughout the Kargil conflict, the Pakistani government continued incessantly to deny its involvement in the operations led by the Mujahideen.

Under such conditions, the Jamaat becomes the instrument of Pakistani policy. Similarly, the Amir of the Jamaat recently appeared in the company of the chief of the Mujahideen while the Pakistani government was denying any involvement. Even with the limited means at its disposal it is able to keep alive a low intensity conflict and therefore keep the issue of Kashmir on the boil without Islamabad ever appearing officially as the instigator of the unrest.

The question of the relations of the Jamaat with the state machinery of Pakistan cannot, however, be reduced to a binary relationship or to a greater or lesser degree of proximity to the party in power. It also reflects the power struggles within the state machinery itself, notably between the Minister for Internal Affairs and the ISI, as is evident in Pakistan's Afghan policy. Benazir Bhutto had been quite simply forbidden by the ISI, during her first term as Prime Minister, from interfering in Afghan affairs, which were considered to be the domain of the secret services alone. The ISI had indeed been able to make remarkable use of the privileged relations maintained by the Jamaat with Afghan Islamists since the mid 1960s. Without becoming the docile instrument of the authorities, the Jamaat had shown itself to be a useful and cooperative ally. From the autumn of 1994, on the other hand, the Home Minister favoured the emergence (and not the creation) of the Taliban, preferring thereafter the conservative option to the Islamist option. The Jamaat found itself, therefore, at loggerheads with government policy though it continued to cooperate with the ISI with which it shared some interests. But while the ISI progressively took control of the *Pakistani action* with regard to the Taliban[73] while supporting its former allies, for ideological reasons the Jamaat supported only Islamist Afghan parties and therefore saw itself marginalized.[74] In Kashmir, on the other hand, it continued to play a significant role. It is interesting to note that the ceasefire proposal of the Hizbul Mujahideen, in August 2000 was in accordance with the unilateral ceasefire along the line of control ordered by General Musharraf.

Similarly, the relative quiescence of the party can be explained by the indecision of the Pakistani authorities in the face of this crisis.

NATURE OF THE BONDS BETWEEN ISLAMIST MOVEMENTS

Should we infer from our analysis so far and from the links that bind the movements all over the world (which meet regularly during large international conferences) that there exists a veritable 'Islamist Internationale'?[75] Even though the Jamaat can put at the disposal of Islamist activists from any region the facilities of military training that it has at its disposal in Pakistan,[76] or even that some of its elements are involved directly in the conflicts affecting the Muslim world,[77] it does not, however, argue the existence of an Islamist equivalent of the Komintern. There is, in fact, no authoritative body which can assume the overall leadership over this macrocosm.[78]

All those holding positions of responsibility in the different Jamaat-i-Islami of the subcontinent insist on the total independence of each Jamaat. Their officials meet, it is true, at international conferences organized by the different components of the Islamic orbit, or, from time to time, in Saudi Arabia, but each of them is an independent party and not an offshoot of the Pakistani Jamaat.[79] Apart from the differences already indicated, the most noteworthy fact in this connection is undoubtedly the total absence of relations between the Jamaat-i-Islami Hind and the Jamaat-i-Islami Jammu Kashmir which hold very different views on the Kashmir issue. The Gulf war is another example of this independence of views. The Jamaat-i-Islami Pakistan was the only one which sided against the allied intervention in Saudi Arabia and in Kuweit.[80] The other Jamaats felt that the threat that Saddam represented to the unity of the Muslim world out weighed every other consideration. The most extreme case remains, however, that of the Jamaat-i-Islami Hind which even disputes the validity of politicization.

This complete autonomy extends to the overall Islamist movements which act alone in their respective national frameworks. Beyond the common aim to achieve re-Islamization, they have no common objectives or strategy. The solidarity achieved between Islamist movements around the Jamaat is functional, circumstantial solidarity and not the manifestation of the unity of a political movement. The Jamaat finds itself, in Pakistan, in the situation of a national Islamist movement supporting other nationalist Islamist movements which it obliges, in a way, 'to pay' for the training offered by making their militants take part in its own battles.

NOTES

1. Olivier Roy, *L'échec de l'Islam politique*, Paris: Le Seuil, 1992, p. 139.
2. Mohammed-Reza Djalili, *Diplomatie islamique: stratégie internationale du Khomeynisme*, Paris: Presses universitaires de France, 1988, p. 17.
3. Ibid.
4. Ibid., p. 56.
5. Ibid., p. 55.
6. Leonard Binder, 'Islam, Ethnicity and the State in Pakistan: An Overview', in Ali Banuazizi and Myron Weiner (eds.), *The State, Religion and Ethnic Politics, Iran and Afghanistan*, Lahore: Vanguard Books, 1987, pp. 259–66, specially p. 263.
7. J.A. Bernard and M. Pochoy, *L'ambition de l'Inde*, Paris: Fondation pour les études de défense nationale, 1988, p. 67. On 23 March 1940, during a session of the Muslim League, Jinnah declared 'It is a dream that Hindus and Muslims can ever evolve a common nationality. . . . The Hindus and Muslims belong to two religious philosophies, social customs, literature. They neither intermarry nor interdine together and indeed they belong to two different civilizations which are based mainly on conflicting ideas and conceptions. Their as-

pects on life and of life are different. . . . They have different epics, different heroes and different episodes, very often the hero of one is the foe of the other and likewise.' Mohammed-Ali Jinnah, quoted in Salahuddin Ahmad Syed, *Foreign Policy of Pakistan: A Critical Study*, Karachi: Comprehensive Book Service, 1996.

8. Mohammed-Reza Djalili, op. cit., p. 58.
9. Mohammed-Ali Jinnah, quoted in Salahuddin Ahmad Syed, op. cit., p. 5.
10. Samina Yasmeen, 'Pakistan's Cautious Foreign Policy', *Survival*, Vol. 36, Summer 1994, pp. 115–33, specially p. 122.
11. Apart from 'the Muslim school', Samina Yasmeen identifies two other important currents of thought. One 'school', called the 'surrender group' by its opponents, asserts that in the unipolar structure dominated by the United States which has succeeded the bipolarity of the Cold War, Pakistan has no choice but to count almost exclusively on Washington on account of the dependence of its armed forces on the superpower and the close economic links between the two states. The second 'school', based on a multipolar vision of the post cold war world, argues in favour of maintaining close relations with the United States due to their mutual interests but recommends that other important players on the international scene also be taken note of so that the American influence is counter balanced and Islamabad can develop relations of partnership and not just of dependence with Washington. See Samina Yasmeen, op. cit., p. 121.
12. The term, used mostly by Indian authors, and too often repeated indiscriminately by Western writers is in truth, a misinterpretation. It underlines the universalist nature of Islam and takes the Hindus back to the 550 years during which the Mughals, who were Muslims, ruled over the Hindu majority in the Indian subcontinent. This would be forgetting, however, that the creation of Pakistan was essentially a backward step due to a reaction to an inverse phenomenon, namely the fear of the Muslim minority of being dominated by the Hindu majority.
13. The Pakistani dictator was quick to understand that the Soviet invasion of Pakistan indeed offered him a heaven sent opportunity to put an end to the Afghan claim on Pushtunistan. He also managed to extricate himself from the political and military stronghold of the Afghan threat which, though manageable in itself would take on a

totally different dimension in the event of a confrontation with India as Pakistan would then run the risk of having to fight on two fronts. What is more, its status as a 'front line country' enabled it to obtain from the United States a disproportionately high economic and military aid in the face of the Afghan and Soviet armies and which served to bridge partially the gap between the Indian and Pakistani levels of armament. Finally, and more importantly, American indulgence enabled it to achieve considerable progress in its nuclear programme for military ends. On this subject see Frédéric Grare, *Le Pakistan face au conflit afghan, 1979–85: au tournant de la guerre froide*, Paris: L'Harmattan, 1997.

14. On this subject see Jessica Stern, 'Pakistan's Jihad Culture', *Foreign Affairs*, Vol. 79, No. 6, pp. 115–26.
15. The Jamaat-i-Islami had just one member in East Pakistan at the time of the 1947 Partition. The movement made a particularly slow advance there. By 1950 it had 13 members and 35 sympathizers. The leadership of the party was aware that its growth in East Pakistan would depend essentially on its capacity to take account of the aspirations of the local people, notably, the frustrations engendered by the economic disparities between the eastern and western wings of the country. The Jamaat was, however, only able to counter the growing alienation in what was to become Bangladesh by renewing its call for Islamic unity. True, it also opposed the regime of Yahya Khan which it accused of having betrayed Islamic ideology, which in turn led to the dilution of Muslim nationalism. The Jamaat leaders considered, nevertheless, that the ethno-cultural Bengali nationalism was only another face of the same problem. The Jamaat then undertook to make an effort towards the maintenance of the territorial integrity of Pakistan, which could only be done if the latter regained its Islamic identity.

    From 1952, *Tarjuman al Quran*, the journal brought out by Mawdudi, opposed the recognition of Bengali as a national language enjoying the same status as Urdu. At the same time it held the Muslim League, totally discredited in East Pakistan, as being responsible for the burgeoning Bengali nationalism, by not having imposed an Islamic constitution, the only factor capable of checking the slide then taking place. In 1956 it changed its strategy and turned actively in favour of an increased economic parity between the two parts of the country and violently castigated the negligence and lack of interest shown to East Pakistan by the central government. It tried, thus, to turn the population away from the temptation to secede. Its action came, however, too late and its influence was too weak for it to bring any significant change in the course of events. The debate was thereafter monopolized by the Awami League and the Muslim League. The repeated calls of the Jamaat for Islamic unity went unheeded and then it entered actively into the struggle against the secessionist guerilla warfare of the Mukti Bahini. It organized the sinister Al Badr militia, composed mostly of members of the student branch of the Jamaat, the Islami Chatro Shango, which was equipped by the Pakistani army. This episode was to affect permanently the position of the Jamaat on the national issue and also its relationship with the Pakistani state, even as it demarcated the limits of its potential interventions in the matter of foreign policy. The Pakistani nation-state became, through its resistance to Bangladeshi secession, a vector of Islamic unity, which it became important to promote each time its international action became confused or seemed to become confused with the cause of the *umma*.

16. The stress here is on the term 'orbit', that is to say, a more or less structured amorphous grouping within which various networks are formed and get dispersed, but without any unity of command and organization.
17. In this sense, the Indian subcontinent can truly be considered to be one of the cultural poles of Islamism.
18. And with good reason. For instance, while the movement of the Muslim Brothers was set up in 1927, the Jamaat-i-Islami made its appearance as a party only in 1940.
19. Without, for all that, breaking its ties with Iran.
20. Olivier Roy, *L'Afghanistan: Islam et modernité politique*, Paris: Le Seuil, 1985, p. 279.
21. This connivance between the Jamaat and the army was not new. It started at the time of the 1970 elections, when the army sought the support of the Jamaat against the Awami League. The Jamaat was defeated in these elections but it set up the Al Badr militia which became a viable ally of the army and it held sway with remarkable violence in East Pakistan, the future Bangladesh. It grew considerably during this period, along with the rise to power of General Hamid Gul within the Inter Service Intelligence (ISI), Pakistan's secret service.

22. Sreedhar and Paul Kapil, 'Politics of Islamic Terrorism in West Asia: Internal and External Dimensions', *Strategic Analysis*, June 1996, Vol. XIX, No. 3, pp. 435–66, specially p. 445.
23. The training camps of the Mujahideen are basically spread over three zones. These are Azad Kashmir, the tribal areas of Baluchistan and NWFP and Afghanistan. The militants, coming from all over the Muslim world, move about from one to the other. They generally receive an initial, relatively short training, which can last up to three months in one area, before being sent for a longer period to another camp where they complete their training which consists, basically, of learning how to handle light arms and explosives. They are then sent to fight in one of the zones of conflict in which Pakistan is directly involved (Afghanistan or Kashmir). They then return to their country of origin where they take part in the fight against the authorities in power, and in the training of their militant colleagues. A typical course, as revealed by two activists, consisted of a three month training course in an Azad Kashmir camp after which they were sent to Khost (Afghanistan) where they remained for six months, learning how to handle explosives. They had then to fight for eighteen months against the men of Najibullah before being sent back to Kashmir at the time of the fall of the Afghan Head of state. They then fought against the Indian forces till they were arrested by the latter.
24. Qazi Hussein Ahmed has repeatedly reiterated his support to Chechen rebels during the course of the year 2000. See Vinod Anand, 'Export of Holy Terror to Chechnya from Pakistan', *Strategic Analysis*, Vol. XXIV, No. 2, June 2000, pp. 539–51, specially p. 548.
25. For an analysis of the involvement of the Jamaat in these conflicts see Astrid Borcke, *Unforeseen Consequences of a Soviet Intervention: The Movement of the Afghans in Militant Islamism*, Koln: Bundesinstitut fur Ostewissenschatliche und Internationale Studien.
26. This assertion is based on interviews with some of those in charge of the Jamaat-i-Islami, Mansoorah, Lahore, conducted in June 1996.
27. Interview with Hamid Gul, former Director of the ISI, Rawalpindi, conducted in August 1993.
28. It dated back in fact, to the failed coup attempt against Daoud in 1975.
29. Particularly Kandahar.
30. Interview with Qazi Hussein Ahmad, Amir Jamaat-i-Islami, Mansoorah, conducted on 16 June 1996.

31. For a historical background to the conflict after the fall of Najibullah, see among other works, Das Gupta, Jyoti Bhasu , 'Afghanistan (1979-1998)' , *Asian Studies*, Vol. XVI, No. 1, January–June 1999, pp. 1–48.
32. Particularly American and British (the latter being accused of wanting to divide Afghanistan into small ethnic-based states) as also French, Massoud being considered the 'instrument' of the latter. Interview with Qazi Hussein Ahmad.
33. Interview with Qazi Hussein Ahmad.
34. The extent of the territories covered by the term Pushtunistan varies considerably, depending on who is the claimant. For the Pushtuns living in Pakistan it only covers the present North-West Frontier Province (NWFP). For Afghan governments prior to the Soviet invasion, it covered this same province as well as Baluchistan. For some Pushtuns living outside Pakistan, Pushtunistan extends from the Indian ocean till Gilgit and from the Durand line to Kashmir. See Kulwand Kaur, *Pak-Afghanistan Relations*, New Delhi: Deep & Deep Publications, 1985, p. 45.
35. In a decree signed on 14 September, he had asserted that Russia's aim was 'the creation of an integrated political and economic community made up of states which can aspire to a position of respect in the world'. The Russian President also asserted that the CIS was, henceforth, a priority zone for Russia on account 'of interests of vital importance' in the fields of 'security, economy and defence of Russians living abroad'. The decree also called for closer economic ties and underlined the need for the formation of a military alliance to set up a system of effective collective defence. *OMRI Daily Digest*, Vol. 1, No. 181, September 1995, p. 1.
36. On Russian objectives in Central Asia, see Irina Zvigeskaia, *The Russian Policy Debate on Central Asia*, London: The Royal Institute of International Affairs, Pinter Publishers, 1995, p. 8.
37. No politico-religious group in Central Asia possesses the frameworks, the social base, the institutional and financial power, or even any plan to be able to truly influence the political processes in the region.
38. Also Turkey and China. I have not dealt with there countries, however, as they are not relevant to the present study.
39. Essentially, Tajikistan.
40. Gas and oil as regards Turkmenistan, oil and cotton as regards Uzbekistan.

41. The situation of Turkmenistan is significant in this respect. The UNOCAL (United States) and Delta Oil (Saudi Arabia) Companies have, in fact, concluded an agreement of a value of around 3 billion dollars for the construction of a gas pipeline connecting Turkmenistan to Pakistan crossing through Afghanistan. The project had been initially negotiated, on the Afghan side, with the Uzbek chief Rashid Dostom and his Tajik counterpart Ismael Khan at Herat. When the latter was made to flee the city by the Taliban, the project was opposed on the ground that the Pakistanis wanted total control over it. The Kabul government made the same claim, but anxious to avoid the concentration of a large source of income in the hands of an opposing party which could, if the situation arose, increase regionalization, decided against the implementation of the project till the very uncertain establishment of a durable peace in the whole country. The project was postponed after the American bombing of Afghanistan in 1996.
42. Around ten Russian technicians were said to be based at Bagram airport where four planes carrying arms, oil or money printed in Moscow land daily, coming from Russia, Tajikistan or the Ukraine. See Rashid Ahmed, *Far Eastern Economic Review*, 1 February 1995. By thus giving their support to the Tajik commandant, the Russians were doing no more than responding to the veiled appeal that the latter had repeatedly been making to them since the failure of the Peshawar agreement of March 1993. The desire to obtain the support of Moscow to regain power in Kabul played a major role in the pressures exerted by Massoud's men at the Tajik border by the side of the 'Islamo-Democratic' forces. See Mohammed-Reza Djalili and Frédéric Grare, 'Le Tadjikistan: convoitises et enjeux régionaux, le rôle de l'Afghanistan, du Pakistan et de l'Iran', in Mohammed-Reza Djalili and Frédéric Grare, *Le Tadjikistan à l'épreuve de l'indépendance*, Geneva: IUHEI, 1995, pp. 121, 134.
43. It is said that the Hezb-i-Islami had already worked for the Russians by using its men to overthrow Elchibey in Azerbaijan. See Michel Barry, 'Kaboul: la mise à mort', *Politique internationale*, No. 64, Summer 1994, pp. 65–96, specially p. 86.
44. The issue of whether this desertion was the result of a calculated choice by the Pakistani government or of a power struggle within it between the ISI and the Minister for Internal Affairs of General Nasrullah Babar, is not relevant to the problematics being considered here.

45. Since July 1994 Islamabad has an extradtion agreement with Cairo for the expulsion of 'Afghans' wanted by Egyptian authorities. Moreover, around 200 Islamist activists were arrested in Pakistan after the attack on the Egyptian Embassy in Islamabad on 19 November 1995. See Astrid Von Borcke, op. cit., pp. 29–30.
46. The support they offered was logistical (arms, training camps, etc.).
47. The man who threatened British and French forces based in Saudi Arabia, Ossama Ben Laden, had taken refuge in Afghanistan, in the Kunar province, controlled by Sayyaf till the arrival of the Taliban. A rich Saudi who owns a large construction enterprise, he is in fact the founder of the party of Sayyaf and he financed all Islamist parties during the war. Belonging to the Saudi royal family, he was expelled from it under American pressure during the Gulf war in which he took part on the side of Iraq. He settled in Yemen before coming to settle in Afghanistan, a few days before the attack against the American forces in Darhan.
48. Where Moscow, which constructed an airport at Taloqan in order to send supplies to him, will help him in all likelihood to strengthen his bases.
49. Moscow hastily convened on 4 October, at Almaty a meeting of the Central Asian republics from which only Turkmenistan was absent. *Le Monde*, Friday, 4 October 1996.
50. This was the only party which fought and suffered heavy losses during the fall of Kabul.
51. Even though Mawdudi had declared, with regard to Kashmir that it was a 'non-*jihad*'. See Sayyed Vali Reza Nasr, *Mawdudi and the Making of Islamic Revivalism*, New York and Oxford: Oxford University Press, 1996.
52. Davis Anthony, 'The conflict in Kashmir', *Jane's Intelligence Review*, Vol. 7, No. 1, 1996, pp. 40–6, specially p. 44. Set up in 1977, the JKLF (presided over today by Yasin Malik) became a credible organization in 1988 when bonds were established between its leader in exile, Amanullah Khan, and the Islamic Student League (ISL), a student movement based in Srinagar. It recruited hundreds of young persons armed for revolt. In 1990 the JKLF led a mass protest campaign in the Valley. It was, however, rapidly overtaken by the Hizbul Mujahideen. Its armed action is today very limited.
53. The Kashmiri territory is today divided between three countries.

45.6 per cent is with India, 35.1 per cent with Pakistan and 19.2 per cent with China.

54. The Jamaat-i-Islami Jammu Kashmir constitutes a unique case in the Jamaat orbit. It cannot be considered to be national Islamism since Jammu and Kashmir is not independent, but its action is deployed, nevertheless, within a Muslim majority population.
55. The Hizbul Mujahideen, reportedly, has close links with the ISI. At the same time, most Hizbul-Mujahideen members are Valley Kashmiris.
56. Interview with Yasin Malik, Chairman of the Jammu and Kashmir Liberation Front, Srinagar, on 1 July 1996.
57. The JKLF and the Jamaat-i-Islami/Hizbul Mujahideen were not, however, the only organizations operating in the province of Jammu & Kashmir. Attempting to reproduce the strategy deployed in Afghanistan, the Pakistanis (in the event the ISI), tried to promote a multiplicity of groups (going up to, it is suggested, 181). Operations were divided between these groups of insurgents operating under diverse names and identities. Through supplies of arms, some of these groups were pushed to the forefront of the political scene. The most prominent among these groups are:

    - The Jammu and Kashmir Liberation Front and the Hizbul Mujahideen, already mentioned.
    - The Harakat-ul-Ansar (Movement of the Companions of the Prophet). Born out of the reunification of two activist organizations (Harakat-ul-Jehad Islami and Harakat-ul-Mujahideen), it is a radical group based in Islamabad. Having about 8,000 members, it has operated, apart from Kashmir, in Tajikistan, Bosnia and the Philippines. One of its branches, Al Faran, was responsible for the kidnapping of five Europeans in July 1995.
    - Harakat-ul-Jihad made up of veterans from Afghanistan. It is said that this outfit is purely a creation of the ISI.
    - Pakistan Special Force. This group is, reportedly, a unit of the ISI whose members operate wearing the Indian uniform, to help Kashmiri combatants during major crises.

    Mention should be made also of the Jamaat-Isla and other less important groups (Janbaz Mujahideen, Ikhwan-ul-Muslimeen, Al-Jihad, Al Barq, Jihad Force, Al-Omar-Mujahideen, Hizbullah, Jamaat-ul-Mujahideen, Tehriq-ul Mujahideen, Allah Tigers, Al-Umar

Commandos, Nassir-ul-Islam, Hizb-i-Islami). See P. Stobdan, 'Kashmir: The Key Issues', *Strategic Analysis*, Vol. XIX, No. 1, pp. 111–39, specially pp. 119–20.

58. This independence with regard to Pakistan should be treated with caution. While it seems correct that the Jamaat-i-Islami of Jammu Kashmir has real functional autonomy, the fact remains that it receives both logistic and financial assistance from Pakistan. The leaders of the Hizbul Mujahideen, the activist branch of the party, go regularly to Mansoorah where they take part in the meetings of the Pakistani Jamaat.
59. Ahmad Mumtaz, 'Islamic Fundamentalism in South Asia: the Jamaat-i-islami and the Tablighi Jamaat of South Asia', in Martin E. Marty and Scott R. Appleby, *Fundamentalisms Observed*, London and Chicago: University of Chicago Press, 1991, p. 506.
60. The Muslim Conference also demands reunification but is politically much less important than the Jamaat-i-Islami, both numerically and within the APHC.
61. The role of the Jamaat in the Kashmir conflict will be discussed later.
62. Which is not to say that the Indian government does not give them cause to do so. The majority of observers are in agreement over the fact that the Indian forces are responsible for most of the deaths occurring in the Valley.
63. P. Stobdan, op. cit., p. 113.
64. The number of 'Arabs' having infiltrated into the Valley should, however, not be exaggerated. By way of example, out of around 561 activists killed, wounded, arrested or simply identified between 1988 and 1994, only 18 were 'Arabs'. Report, *Involvement of Pakistan in Jammu and Kashmir*, New Delhi: IDSA, 1994. The argument of 'Arab mercenaries' constitutes, above all, a facile argument used by some governments (notably that of Pakistan) to absolve themselves of responsibility.
65. P. Stobdan, op. cit., p. 113.
66. The different journals controlled by the Jamaat in Great Britain regularly publish appeals for funds meant, officially, for humanitarian aid in Kashmir. Questioned by the author about the final destination of this money, Syed Ali Shah Gilani, Chairman of the political Bureau of the Jamaat-i-Islami Jammu Kashmir refused to give a reply. *Interview*, Srinagar, 1 July 1996.
67. The Hizbul Mujahideen, for its part, conducts its recruitment

in accordance with other criteria. It scouts for members during anti-Indian demonstrations which take place regularly in the Valley. The most active and the most physically robust elements are then enrolled into the ranks of the party. They are then sent to Azad Kashmir to undergo preliminary training in the handling of arms and explosives, followed by a stay in an Afghan camp and often by a period of actual fighting in Afghanistan, or at the Tajik border. Based on interviews conducted with some militants of the Hizbul Mujahideen in Srinagar on 2 July 1996.

68. Estimates vary according to sources between 5 and 20 per cent, the latter figure originating, naturally, from the Jamaat itself. The reality seems closer, however, to 10 per cent
69. Some militants of the Jamaat-i-Islami (mainly the youth) have even declared to the author that they desire the independence of Kashmir and not its unification with Pakistan. Whatever the truth however there is still a deep alienation from New Delhi.
70. In spite of settling of scores and other assassinations within it.
71. Though some express their doubts over its viability.
72. Practically all the victims of the Indian forces, or 'renegades' are members or sympathizers of the Jamaat. 'Renegades' are former rebels who, having been forced into a 'change of heart' by the Indian forces, through torture as well as by being bought off (although no renegade will ever admit this, preferring to invoke ideological or/and humanitarian motives), have grouped together as an independent militia to fight Kashmiri insurgents. Having fought within different resistance groups whose bases and strategy they are aware of, they constitute a particularly valuable element of power for the Indian forces who are thus exonerated from the responsibility of a number of killings and other atrocities.
73. And not the Taliban itself.
74. It continues, nonetheless, to try to play a role on the Afghan scene by attempting to bring the parties together. The Taliban are, however, extremely mistrustful of it and Qazi Hussein Ahmad has so far only met with refusals. Interview with Mulla Mohammed Hassan, Governor of Kandahar conducted on 25 November 1996.
75. Though a number of observers currently hold an opposite view. See, particularly, the article by Jean-Jacques Lavenue, 'Sur la formation d'une internationale islamiste: la Conférence populaire islamique de Khartoum et la pensée d'Hassan El-Tourabi', *Revue de*

la recherche juridique, Droit prospectif, Aix Marseille: Presses Universitaires d'Aix Marseille, No. 1, 1996, pp. 39--64.

76. Though it is not alone in controlling these facilities.
77. Representatives of the overall countries of the Maghreb, Tunisians, Algerians, etc., are to be found in the Islamic University of Islamabad, shifting from one institution to another, controlled by the Jamaat-i-Islami. The Jamaat gives political support to the most radical movements and trains their combatants in its camps. The Jamaat is also suspected of helping some Islamist circles in Isareli-occupied territories. It should, however, be noted that the Jamaat or its Afghan allies are by no means the only ones to adopt such tactics. Besides, those in charge, particularly from the FIS, and from the different Islamist movements operating in this region, have regular contacts with the Jamaat during international conferences organized by the latter. The Jamaat, however, seems, for obvious reasons,to be more attracted towards two countries, Algeria and Bosnia. The writings of the Jamaat are fairly discreet with regard to Algeria but some Algerian extremists have availed of the military training given by the Hezb-i-Islami of Hekmatyar. The involvement of the Jamaat in Bosnia seems, on the other hand, more marked. Throughout 1995, Jamaat publications talked at length of the Bosnian tragedy, underlining the insufficiency of the assistance given to the government of Alija Izetbegovic by Muslim countries and even more, the duplicity of Western governments. *Impact International* wrote in August 1995: 'It is now increasingly clear that the apparent tomfoolery of the "blue helmets" in Bosnia the whole world has been witnessing on television screens is not the result of disunity in the international community, ineptitude or lack of determination to stop Serbian aggressors. It is a carefully planned operation concocted by London and Paris to deceive the world while the real intention is to help the Serbian side to victory.' Through its parliamentary representation the party of Qazi Hussein Ahmad, repeatedly called on the Pakistani government to give military support to the Bosnians. The Jamaat-i-Islami Pakistan, as also the overall Jamaats of the subcontinent sent not only money to the Bosnian government but also trained Bosnian combatants in its Afghan and Pakistani camps. Some Pakistani members of the Jamaat are also said to have fought in Bosnia by the side of the men of Alija Izetbegovic, as testified by a conversation this author had with some officials of the Jamaat at

Mansoorah in Lahore in June 1996. Estimates of the number of Pakistani members of the Jamaat who fought in Bosnia vary, ranging from ten to more than a hundred. The Amir of the Jamaat, Qazi Hussein Ahmad himself went to Bosnia in 1995.

78. This relates, obviously, only to the Sunni movements.
79. With the exception of the Jamaat of Azad Kashmir which receives its instructions from Lahore.
80. And not in favour of Saddam Hussein, as is sometimes assumed.

5. The Jamaat-i-Islami and Minority Islam

The Jamaat-i-Islami has evolved in a very different fashion in the countries where Islam is in the minority. The claim for a political Islam has given way, both in discourse as in practice, to the assertion of an identity. In countries where Islam is sociologically predominant, the Jamaat-i-Islami got grounded in conserving the heritage of Mawdudi's original way of thinking. In countries where Muslims constitute a minority, the Jamaat kept concentrated on the preservation of the rights of the Muslim community. This protection was not, however, devoid of a certain degree of openness to the culture and the living conditions of the majority. Therefore, it was susceptible to modernity. The challenge before the Jamaat was, therefore, to conserve the cultural and ideological heritage of Mawdudi while being receptive to modernity. But it is not the least among the paradoxes of the history of the Jamaat, and undoubtedly its greatest frustration, that it is precisely because it was able to modernize technologically as well as culturally, that it cut itself off from its own community and could not monopolize the representation of the Muslim diaspora scattered all over the world.

THE JAMAAT-I-ISLAMI HIND

In August 1947, at the time of Partition, only 240 members out of the 999 that the Jamaat was then composed of, remained in India.[1] In April 1947, when Partition seemed imminent, Mawdudi had declared in a speech in Madras that the Jamaat should be divided into an Indian and a Pakistani organization, each working within its own respective political structure. This original split led to much more than a simple partition of the organization. It became a veritable ideological split. It was not the result of a long and painful intellectual debate, but the inevitable consequence of different conditions of existence. Under the impetus of Mawdudi, the Jamaat-i-Islami Pakistan was converted into a veritable political party and soon became the nerve centre of the movement. The conquest of the state being thereafter its main objective, it was soon completely separated from the Indian branch of the movement which evolved thereafter in an environment in which Muslims represented no more than 11 per cent of the population.

The Jamaat was, in this sense, recreated in April 1948 in a meeting in Allahabad where the 240 members who had remained in India, met. The party which then took up the name of Jamaat-i-Islami Hind, declared itself independent from any other organization. It, thus, resolved to distance itself from the Jamaat-i-Islami Pakistan and to assert its resolutely Indian character. The Jamaat-i-Islami Hind refused thereafter to participate in elections.[2] Functioning in a secular environment, it had to give up any claim to establishing some day an Islamic state in India.[3]

Two issues were to dominate the JIH, nationalism and secularism. On the first point, reiterating Mawdudi's initial position, the JIH exhorted Muslims to turn their backs on nationalism in all its forms and to accept the sole guidance of Islam which prohibits the pursuit of all sectarian interests. The JIH also firmly opposed, but not without some ambiguity, the secular nature of the state. In the perception of the Jamaat, the modern secular state was based on the negation .of the sovereignty of God. Consequently, the state and not God became the source of ethical law. Not having the attributes of justice and of infallibility, the secular state could not establish the rule of justice within its own borders, hence tyranny, injustice and finally war. For the Jamaat, the remedy lay in the acceptance of the doctrine of the sovereignty of God and the supremacy of divine law in all spheres of life.[4] At the same time, however, the Jamaat saw in the secular nature of the Indian state the surest guarantee of the continued existence of Islam in India.[5] The JIH, in fact, established a clear distinction between secularism as an atheist ideology which had to be fought against, and secularism as a state policy, enshrined in the Constitution, which obliged the state to abstain from all discrimination or partiality on the basis of religious convictions. This latter concept was naturally, acceptable to the Jamaat.

With 4,000 members and some 25,000 workers functioning in fourteen distinct zones, the Jamaat-i-Islami Hind devotes most of its energy to safeguarding the cultural and religious identity of Indian Muslims. The question of communalism is a major preoccupation in this connection and reflects the growing anxiety of a population that is largely in a minority in a country where religious nationalism is growing day by day. Thus, the main objective of the Forum for Democracy and Communal Amity (FDCA), an organization set up by the Jamaat to fight communalism, is to 'arouse public conscience against the rising tide of aggressive communalism and fascism and a sense of social accountability at the individual and collective levels'; to make efforts 'for the eradication of communal riots and for the rehabilitation of victims of such unfortunate happenings' and to 'compile proposals at legal and administrative levels to contain communal and fascist forces and to make serious efforts for their implementation by the administration'.[6] The Indian Jamaat has, thus, allied itself with other Muslim, as also ecumenical organizations, to promote harmony and national unity in a multi-racial, multi-linguistic and multi-cultural Indian society.[7]

But the Jamaat-i-Islami Hind does not restrict itself to formulating a defence of the Muslim community. It also attempts to 'build the character'of Muslims, a *sine qua non* of the projection of their identity in non-Muslim circles, which is the second constituent of its mission. In this respect, the action of the Jamaat is mainly of a social and religious nature. Programmes imparting religious education, the defence of the rights of Muslims, of Urdu and of Muslim educational institutions are the most tangible components of a programme which is, above all, a call to individuals to strengthen their faith.[8]

The Jamaat also strives to foster a spirit of unity among different sections and schools of thought and to impress upon Muslims the need to solve their problems jointly in accordance with Islamic principles. It pays due attention to all important problems of the community which are indispensable for its very existence and for the preservation of its cultural identity such as, for example, religious education and Muslim Personal Law. It also aims at imparting basic moral and religious education to the younger generations so that they become 'trustees of their Faith, servants of their community and builders of their country'.[9]

In spite of its opposition to the Pakistani project, however, the JIH is suspected by Indian circles of promoting a 'separatist' community. As Violette Graff points out, the Jamaat 'will only rarely succeed in surmounting the hostility that its Islamic rigidity arouses in the Indian milieu'.[10]

Its major problem, however, lies probably less in this Islamic rigour than in the constantly latent suspicion against it, as against the Muslim community as a whole in India, of being a sort of 'fifth column' at the service of Pakistan. This situation forces it incessantly to justify itself and provokes it to adopt, on a number of issues, attitudes that are radically contrary to those of its Pakistani counterpart. Desirous of gaining recognition of its status as a Muslim Indian community, it has constantly supported India's membership of the Organization of Islamic Conference (OIC),[11] to which the Pakistani Jamaat is opposed. The same desire leads it to militate in favour of an improvement of relations between India and Pakistan so that all sources of tension having a national-religious connotation can be eliminated. On Kashmir, finally, it supports autonomy for the Valley within the framework of the Indian federal state. This position brings it radically in opposition to the Jamaat-i-Islami Jammu Kashmir and the Pakistani Jamaat. In line with its positions on secularism, the Jamaat-i-Islami Hind has established a clear distinction between the Pakistani nation state and the Muslim nation,[12] a mythical, ideal nation with no political connotations. It is this latter and this alone which engages the attention of the Jamaat. It is also this which singles it out and distinguishes it from the other Jamaats of the subcontinent.

THE DIASPORA: THE CASE OF GREAT BRITAIN

The foothold that the Jamaat-i-Islami has established in various countries of the world is the work of its subcontinental diaspora. It is, thus, strongly represented in South Africa, the United States (through the Islamic Circle of North America) and to a lesser degree, in a number of European countries where Muslims from the subcontinent are found. Its importance in each of these countries is proportional to the size of its community, though the entire community cannot be totally identified with the Jamaat-i-Islami.

Of all the countries of Europe, Great Britain definitely has the largest number of Islamic groups originating in the subcontinent. Indian Muslims, Bangladeshis and Pakistanis constitute the majority in a Muslim community there and members are placed between 1.2 and 2 million.[13] The Jamaat-i-Islami has strong roots in this community where it has been able to develop a closely-knit network of organizations. It is represented in all the cities of the United Kingdom having a substantial Muslim population, like Manchester, Birmingham, Wolverhampton, Southampton, etc.

The situation of the Muslims of Great Britain constitutes a

unique case in Europe. The assertion of the Islamic identity there takes place within a multicultural concept of society 'conceived as the juxtaposition of "minorities" and of "communities" which are the guardians of the political identity of their members and the chosen intermediaries of their integration in their relationships with the State'.[14] This communalism constitutes the central element of the strategy of the Jamaat-i-Islami in Great Britain. Though, it is strongly denounced by the Mawdudist organization it constitutes a necessary stage in a strategy of conquest, aimed at surpassing itself.[15]

The activity of the majority of the Muslim organizations[16] in Great Britain centres around the second and third generations of Muslim immigrant workers (whose parents or grandparents had come from the Indian subcontinent) and to their more or less conscious break from the native homeland. First generation immigrants coming from the Indian subcontinent continued with political allegiances they had made in the motherland. In this sense, the British Jamaat was hardly any more than a projection of the Pakistani or Bangladeshi Jamaats. The political affiliations of subsequent generations, on the other hand, were with local parties and the bond with the country of origin became much looser. The first generation, persuaded to return to the mother country after having put by a little money earned in England, had hardly presented any problems, as it continued to harken back and to pay the *zakat*. With subsequent generations, on the other hand, the question of national identity and even more of religious identity, became a problem. Muslim organizations, particularly the Jamaat (which had profited widely from the manna supplied by the collection of the *zakat*) made it their main objective to disseminate a greater knowledge of Islam within the Muslim community and above all to help the young to conserve and shoulder their Muslim identity in a Western environment. For the Muslim Educational Trust for example, it was a matter of 'safeguarding and defending the separate Muslim identity in children exposed to the permissive Western society, characterized in the first place by the surge of publications of an obscene nature' as also by 'broken families, sexual promiscuity, alcoholism and loose morals'.[17]

The Jamaat-i-Islami does not propose, however, to confine itself to the role of champion of the community. It wants to project to the non-Muslim majority an image of modernity, that of an Islam in step with the times, intransigent, true, as regards ethics and culture but shouldering and integrating totally the intellectual and technological heritage of the century. The Islamic Foundation, for instance, carries on important teaching and research activities. This makes of it a sort of laboratory for the Jamaat. Economics figures at the top of its preoccupations. Linked to various economic and financial institutions in the Muslim world the Foundation tries to propagate its own concept of international economy by organizing seminars and working groups. It is to this end that it has recently tied up with the Loughborough University of Technology for the teaching of Islamic economics. The students attend courses there for a little more than a year to obtain a Master of Science degree which could, if required, lead to a doctorate. Apart from 'classical' economics courses, they receive training in the principles of Islamic economics and finance, a large part of which relates to the 'comprehension and management of financial and monetary institutions working without rates of interest'.[18]

The Jamaat has not succeeded in Great Britain, any more than in the rest of the world, in extricating itself from the ethnic, national or even social factors weighing on it. The distribution of 'spheres of influence' between organizations took place quickly and very naturally along ethnic and national lines. In spite of its universalist message and its proclaimed resolve to spread the message of Islam among non-believers,[19] the Islamic Mission of the United Kingdom focusses most of its activities on the subcontinental community.[20] This orientation is still more marked in the Dawatul Islam whose ethnic character formed the very basis of its creation. The ethnic factor is not absent from the Islamic Foundation of Leicester either, most of whose leaders are themselves of subcontinental origin. Its activities target, it is true, a much wider public covering the overall British Muslim community, as also the entire *ummah* whose creation the foundation wishes to spearhead in its march towards the twenty-first century.[21]

This distinction between the institutions coming within the orbit of the Jamaat is marked both by their ability in a particular language as by their ability to use the tools of modernity. While Urdu seems[22] to have remained the primary language spoken within the Islamic Mission, English is the main medium of communication of the Islamic Foundation. This use of English for its publications as a whole enables it to 'communicate its message in the universal dominant language and to contest the Western "secular" cultural hegemony, on its own linguistic soil'.[23] This makes the Islamic Foundation of Leicester one of the major centres today for the spread of militant Sunni Islamist thought.[24] Similarly, while the former makes use only of the written word, the latter also uses software and all modern means of communication.[25]

NOTES

1. M.S. Agwani, *Islamic Fundamentalism in India*, Chandigarh: Twenty-First Century India Society, 1986, p. 61.
2. Interview with officials in charge of the Jamaat-i-Islami Hind, New Delhi.
3. No reference to this subject appears in its political programme. In its 1990–4 programme, it is stated that 'the Jamaat can take part in elections, at the opportune time and in consonance with its principles' but this statement has disappeared from the preface of the 1995–9 programme. *Policy and Programme, April 1995–March 1999*, Jamaat-i-Islami Hind, New Delhi.
4. M.S. Agwani, op. cit., p. 68.
5. Ahmad Mumtaz, 'Islamic Fundamentalism in South Asia: the Jamaat-

i-islami and the Tablighi Jamaat of South Asia', in Martin E. Marty and Scott R. Appleby, *Fundamentalisms Observed*, London and Chicago: University of Chicago Press, 1991, p. 505.

6. *Forum for Democracy and Communal Amity*, New Delhi, 1999.
7. Ahmad Mumtaz, op. cit., p. 504.
8. See *Policy and Programme, April 1995-March 1999*, New Delhi: Jamaat-i-Islami Hind, 1995.
9. *Jamaat-I-Islami Hind: An Introduction*, Jamia Nagar, New Delhi: Jamaat-i-Islami Hind, Abul Fazl Enclave.
10. Violette Graff, 'La Jamaat-i-Islami Hind', in Carre Olivier and Dumont Paul, op. cit., pp. 77–99, specially p. 79.
11. On the issue of the relations between India and this organization, see A.K. Pasha, *India and OIC, Strategy and Diplomacy*, New Delhi: Centre for Peace Studies, 1995.
12. Ahmad Mumtaz, op. cit., p. 504.
13. The actual figure is probably nearer 1.2 million. See on this subject, Jorgen S. Nielsen, *Muslims in Western Europe*, Edinburgh: Edinburgh University Press, 1992, p. 45 and Ceri Peach, 'The Muslim Population of Great Britain', *Ethnic and Racial Studies*, Vol. 13, No. 3, July 1990.
14. Gilles Kepel, *A l'Ouest d'Allah*, Paris: Le Seuil, 1994, p. 148.
15. Of the organizations controlled by the Jamaat, five are important: These are the Islamic Foundation of Leicester, the Islamic Mission of the United Kingdom with its headquarters in London, the 'Muslim Education Trust', the Dawatul Islam and the organization of the 'Young Muslims of the United Kingdom'.

    - Founded in 1973, the Islamic Foundation of Leicester is a non-government organization with educational objectives. The Islamic Foundation controls more than twenty centres throughout the country. These centres encompass generally a mosque, a Koranic school and a community centre. The most important of these is in Sparkbrook, Birmingham, where more than a thousand children regularly receive religious education. The Foundation also maintains bonds of cooperation in the fields of education, research and publications with various universities of the world. Mention can be made, notably, of the International Islamic University of Malaysia, the Islamic Foundation of Bangladesh, the Ulhman de Fodio University, Sohoto (Nigeria), the International Islamic University of Islamabad and the International

University of Africa, located in the Sudan. Finally, the link between the Islamic Foundation and Saudi Arabia is strong. The Director of Public Relations of the Foundation goes regularly on visits to the Saudi kingdom as also the Executive Director who participates equally regularly in conferences which are held there.

- Founded in 1962, the Islamic Mission of the United Kingdom has around thirty-five branches all over the British territory. Among the notable centres are in Crawley, South London, Reading, Slough, Southampton, Woking, Cardiff, Lampeter, Nottingham, Sheffield, Huddersfield, Liverpool and Stockton-on-Tees. It is said to control the largest network of mosques in the country. Its structure is quite identical with that of the Jamaat-i-Islami. The Islamic Mission accepts members under the category of sympathizers, associate members and members. These categories are defined as follows:

  –Members: those who submit to the discipline of the Mission;
  –Associate Members: those who subscribe to the Mission's ideas and cooperate with in its multifarious activities;
  –Sympathizers: Those who sympathise with the cause of the Mission.

- Set up in 1966 by the Islamic Mission of the United Kingdom and led by a Bangladeshi academic, the Muslim Education Trust, specialises in organizing contacts with schools so as to enable Muslim students to receive a religious education outside regular school hours. It, thus, controls a network of more than fifty schools across the entire country.
- The Dawatul Islam was born in 1976 as a result of the tension between Pakistanis and Bangladeshis following the separation of Bangladesh.
- The Young Muslims of the United Kingdom operates on university campuses and Polytechnics throughout the country. Its structure and organization is identical to that of the Islamic Mission of the United Kingdom. In the manner of the Jamiat-ul-Tulaba in Pakistan, Young Muslims seems, in fact, to operate as a recruiting organization, channelling the educated Muslim youth of the country towards the Islamic Mission.

This last point postulates the matter of the social base of the recruitment of the Jamaat-i-Islami in Great Britain. There is not enough data available on this subject and it is therefore right to be cautious but it would seem that the choice of the Jamaat, both in Pakistan and in the United Kingdom, is guided by the same type of elitism. The educated urban middle/lower class of the Muslim population constitutes the chosen field of the Jamaat in both countries. The Young Muslims of the United Kingdom, for instance, makes its recruitment, basically, from among the students. Few workers are found among its members.

All these organizations maintain extremely close links between themselves (although the Dawatul Islam is relatively marginalized). They also keep constant contact with the different Jamaat-i-Islami in the Indian subcontinent. Out of nine leaders of the Islamic Foundation identified, six have direct links with the Jamaat-i-Islami, either in Pakistan, or in Bangladesh. Kurham Murad, Executive Director of the Islamic Foundation till 1986, is today an eminent member of the Jamaat in Pakistan. So is Ahmed Kurshid, the number two in the party. Manazir Ahsan, the present Executive Director of the Foundation is a former worker of the Jamaat-i-Islami Bangladesh. These personal bonds do not, however, alter radically the differences in objectives which keep the Pakistani or Bangladeshi Jamaats and their sister organizations distant from each other. They simply reflect the phenomenon of globalization which Olivier Roy talks about, which is displayed in the 'contemporary supranationalism, the internationalization of the network of circulation of ideas, men, goods, not so much in the content as in the transformation of all the content that this cosmopolitanism involves'. The membership of any one of these associations does not preclude, for example, the possibility of being a member of another association. A number of employees of the Islamic Foundation of Leicester, thus, figure in the registers of the Islamic Mission of the United Kingdom. The Executive Director of the Islamic Foundation of Leicester, Manazir Ahsan, is said also to be a member of the Dawatul Islam. Of Bangladeshi origin, holding a doctorate from the School of Oriental and African Studies (SOAS), he is reportedly a former member of the Jamaat-i-Islami Bangladesh. He is, moreover, said to be connected by marriage to the family of Ahmed Kurshid, the number two in the Pakistani Jamaat and President of the

Islamic Foundation of Leicester. Generally, the workers and leaders maintain constant contact with each other. Besides, these organizations sometimes work for each other. A number of events are organized jointly by these organizations, their respective office bearers being regularly invited to address the gatherings at the time of the numerous conferences organized by one or the other among them.

Finally, the literature distributed by these organizations (particularly that of the Islamic Foundation of Leicester and the Islamic Mission of the United Kingdom as literature from the other organizations was not available) is a literature originating essentially from the Jamaat itself, or of the Wahabite trend. The writings of Mawdudi and the other members of the Jamaat occupy a large place in it. The absence of works of Shia theology, or of Sufism, is also significant. In fact, most organizations mentioned here are organizations for conducting the propaganda of the Jamaat-i-Islami in Europe. Their objectives are expressed as follows:

'Demonstrating to the nation's opinion formers, academics, industrialists, financiers, etc., that Islam is a timeless and relevant problem-solving way of life.' To this end, the Mission regularly organizes seminars, training sessions and distributes abundant literature on the Muslim faith. 'Providing valued Islamic Education to Muslim children living in the UK.' Indeed, education constitutes an important component of the activities of the Mission. It, thus, controls 26 evening schools and other 'week-end schools'. In 1980 it established a Central Education Committee to work towards a state school whose courses would be compatible with the national curriculum. Its own curriculum is basically meant to enable students to acquire sufficient mastery over Urdu and over the corpus of Islamic knowledge. This is a pointer to the real objective of the Mission which aims more at controlling the Muslim population of the Indian subcontinent than at spreading the message of Islam to non-believers.

16. Very few organizations have appeared recently which are not linked with immigration. This is the case, particularly, with the 'Muslim Parliament' which groups together British citizens who have converted to Islam.
17. Gilles Kepel, op. cit., p. 167.

18. *To Study Islamic Economics and Finance at a British University*, Loughborough University of Technology, Department of Economics, in cooperation with the Islamic Foundation, Leicester, UK.
    Publication of scholarly works also figures on the top of its agenda. It is because of its publications that the institution has acquired most of its international reputation. The *Muslim Book Review* and the *Index of Islamic Literature*, published jointly with the International Institute for Islamic Thought in Washington, DC, are till now the most complete and the most useful references for international Islamist literature. Apart from classical literature, the Foundation also puts at the disposal of its 'clients' a large amount of audio-visual material (video cassettes, video games, computer software) to spread its message. This activity is reputed to procure for the Foundation a large part of its revenues. Because of the large Muslim population in the world and the quality of the products offered, it does, in fact command a large market. However, according to Ahmed Andrews, who worked at the Islamic Foundation in 1987–8, the sale of its publications will never generate any profit for the Foundation, most of whose financing comes from the Rabitah. Andrews Ahmed, *Jamaat-i-Islami in the UK: A Sociological Study*, op. cit., p. 13.
19. *Annual Report, 1 July 94–30 June 95*, The UK Islamic Mission.
20. At a meeting with an official of the Mission in charge of the propagation of the faith, the author was surprised to note that the official spoke English with great difficulty, which argued, to say the least, against his ability to carry out his functions efficiently.
21. *The Islamic Foundation, Objectives, Activities, Projects*, U.K., Leicester: Islamic Foundation, p. 2.
22. The author remained for too short a while with representatives of the Islamic Mission to make any but very cursory generalizations.
23. Gilles Kepel, *A l'ouest d'Allah*, Paris: Le Seuil, 1994, p. 198.
24. Ibid.
25. Though one cannot deny the simplistic and superficial elements that this classification may contain, it helps to comprehened the developments and trends that the evolution of the Jamaat's universe is undergoing in Great Britain.

6. Neo-Fundamentalism and Globalization: The Rushdie Affair

More than any other event, the controversy which broke out at the end of the eighties following the publication of Salman Rushdie's *The Satanic Verses*, was a pointer to the objectives, the manner of working and the real extent of the influence of the Jamaat-i-Islami. From 26 September 1988, the date of publication of *The Satanic Verses*, till the *fatwa* of Ayatollah Khomeiny on 14 February 1989, the Jamaat played a predominant role in mobilizing anti-Rushdie sentiment and in its ideological rationalization, that is to say in the words of Emilie René, in the creation of a 'world protest' and a 'commonality of interpretation'.[1] It was the first in Europe to spark off an outcry and to attempt, with the help of Saudi Arabia, to mobilize the Muslim world as a whole. In fact, its wide ranging activism in all directions led to the belief in the existence of a vast, organized, powerful and ideologically united international network, the vanguard of a global Muslim society. A close examination of the facts shows, however, a more modest reality. The 'Rushdie Affair' in effect broke out only with the *fatwa* issued by Khomeiny, which by itself brings to light the limits of the Mawdudist party. However, it played a not negligible role in creating conditions that were likely to promote discord though one cannot but note that in its initial phase it had no impact outside the borders of the United Kingdom.[2] It was the death sentence pronounced on the author for apostasy which turned it, in the eyes of the Western world, or at least a part of Western intellectuals, into a veritable conflict of civilizations, between the secular West and the Muslim East, and lent it its international dimension.[3] Analysis brings out, once again, the weak links between the different components of the Jamaat. The 'Rushdie Affair' in its initial phase, was essentially the work of the neo-fundamentalist movement in countries where Islam is by far in the minority, which in no way prevented its being made use of by Muslim states, particularly Saudi Arabia. 'The Affair', once triggered, also had repercussions in Pakistan but the events that took place there were a consequence of the international mobilization in which the Jamaat-i-Islami Pakistan played no dynamic role. It was only because some of its most eminent members also belonged to the Islamic Foundation of Leicester that this confusion was fuelled.

THE AFFAIR

The controversy over *The Satanic Verses* began even before the official publication of the work in London on 26 September 1988. In mid-September two Indian magazines, *India Today* and *Sunday*, published some extracts from the work as well as a series of interviews with the author. Two Muslim representatives of the Indian parliament, Syed Shahabudin and Khurshid Alam, started a campaign to have the work banned in India. It being election campaign time in India, Rajiv Gandhi saw in it the opportunity to gain the sympathy of some 70 million Indian Muslims. On 5 October 1988, the Indian Ministry of Finance placed a ban on the work.[4] The action then shifted towards Great Britain. Even before the ban in India, Aslam

Ejaz of the Islamic Foundation of Madras, itself a branch of the Jamaat-i-Islami Hind, sent the controversial extracts of the work to one of his friends in the Islamic Foundation of Leicester, warning him of the ban imminent on the work and asking him to perform his duty as a believer.[5] On 3 October, the Islamic Foundation of Leicester sent some extracts from the book to Muslim organizations, mosques and ambassadors of Muslim countries in Great Britain. Those in charge of Penguin publications were contacted with the request that the work be immediately withdrawn.[6] On 11 October a United Kingdom Committee for Action on Islamic Affairs was formed in London to mobilize public opinion against this 'sacrilegious and unwarranted attack on the Islamic sanctities'.[7] This committee, which is still active, was officially led at the time by Mughram Al Ghamdi, a Saudi diplomat who was also the Director of the Islamic Cultural centre.[8] It also included, apart from the Islamic Foundation of Leicester, the Islamic Mission of the United Kingdom, the Union of Muslim Organizations, the Council of Mosques (Great Britain and Eire), the Islamic Cultural Centre of London and the Central Mosque Trust, both subsidized by Saudi Arabia. It was on 14 January 1989 that the Bradford demonstration took place during which a copy of the work in question was burnt. On 14 February 1989, finally, that Ayatollah Khomeiny declared in his famous *fatwa* that Rushdie being an apostate, deserved to be put to death while the Iranian state drew up a 'contract' against the author. The Rushdie affair then took on a truly international dimension.

THE LOCAL DIMENSION: THE CASE OF GREAT BRITAIN

If, as Emilie René writes, the Rushdie affair cannot be explained by the single 'approach of mobilizing immigrants through local and national contexts',[9] one cannot ignore this factor either for this local and national dimension constituted the point at which the action of the Jamaat was anchored to reality, without which this action would have been nothing but a hollow discourse without social significance. It was, indeed, the Muslim community in Great Britain and not the non-Muslim majority of the United Kingdom which the Jamaat targeted when it launched 'the affair'. It hoped to be able to draw within its fold, for its benefit, the influence of traditional religious leaders of eminence and to expand in such a way as to include segments of the Muslim community which had, till then, remained outside it, notably the working class population.[10] It was, in fact, Pakistani workers who had become victims of the textile crisis which was then affecting the north of England, who were the first to respond to 'the affair'. Some 30 to 50 per cent of the working population of Pakistani origin was out of work as against 11 per cent of the English population.[11]

The crisis was, hence, an economic one but it was coupled with a crisis of identity for these workers who were often victims of racist attacks without having any appropriate legal recourse available to them. It was these workers who organized the Bradford demonstration of 14 January 1989 during which a copy of *The Satanic Verses* was burnt.[12] The Rushdie affair was going to be, for them, a heaven sent opportunity to finally get themselves recognized by their society of adoption. It is, moreover, symptomatic that the Rushdie affair should have broken out in countries where Muslims were in a minority. It was in India and not in Pakistan that the scandal started. It was in Great Britain that it assumed its full magnitude before reaching the United States where the main vector of the anti-Rushdie campaign was the Islamic Circle of North America, the American branch of the Jamaat-i-Islami, followed soon thereafter by the Islamic Society of North America, which was close to the Mawdudist party but not exclusively controlled by it. Finally, South Africa was among the very first countries to ban the work, well before the large majority of Muslim countries.

This phenomenon is easily explained if we consider that

the central point of the debate around *The Satanic Verses* was the fact that the residents of a brothel mentioned in the book have the same names as the wives of the Prophet. As Jean-Francois Clément writes, 'Some Muslims have concluded from this that, since Muslims were advised to identify themselves with these women, one of whom at least was usually shown as being perfect, it was therefore being asked of their wives that they should be "whores". Another criticism: since the wives of the Prophet are often presented as "mothers of the Muslims" that would mean that all Muslims are "sons of whores".'[13] Undoubtedly 'this fantastical perception takes us back more to the problem of those who construe these meanings than to Rushdie's book',[14] but these interpretations reveal, also, the susceptibility of those who make them. It is therefore only to be expected that the most powerful mobilization should have taken place in countries where Islam is very much in the minority.

AN ANTI-WEST COMPONENT?

There is no better way to define the relation that the Jamaat has, in its neo-fundamentalist manifestation, with the West than through these few lines taken from an introductory brochure of the Islamic Foundation of Leicester which says: 'Western civilization still dominates the world. No part of the world is free from its influence. Everywhere Muslims must successfully face the cultural challenge of the West if they are to succeed in establishing Islam in their land.'[15] These lines take one back to the classical Islamic theory of international relations, already quoted earlier, which makes a distinction between the *Dar al-Islam*, the Muslim space where the precepts of Islam prevail, and the *Dar al-harb* which 'encompasses the countries where Muslim law does not have its effects and whose inhabitants have refused to convert to Islam'.[16] Shorn of its rhetoric, the *Dar al-harb* here refers to countries where the Muslim law is not effective, not because their inhabitants have refused to convert to Islam but because Western influence has made them turn away from its practice or has perverted them. It is, therefore, made up of Muslim countries where the state legitimizes its action through an imported ideology (socialism, liberalism, etc.) and where there is need to establish Islam in order to institute a truly Muslim society as well as the Muslim diaspora, or, more precisely, minority Muslim communities[17] scattered all over the world whose identity needs incessantly to be reasserted on pain of seeing it lose itself within the surrounding culture, often the Western culture. In both cases, the fight is essentially cultural even though it can change into a military confrontation if the governments in power do not simply oppose the Islamist parties but try to eliminate them (physically, if necessary) from the political field, as has been the case in Algeria, Egypt or Tajikistan.

It is from this perspective that the Rushdie affair should be viewed when looking at the action of the Jamaat. The Jamaat and its Saudi allies confined themselves, to begin with, to demanding through conventional legal means, the withdrawal of a work considered to be offensive, by taking recourse to British legislation[18] and jurisprudence. The United Kingdom Committee for Action on Islamic Affairs asked for the total withdrawal of the sale of a work considered blasphemous, apologies from the author and the payment of damages to a Muslim charitable organization in Great Britain.[19] The death threats, which were already being made to Salman Rushdie during this period, came from individuals and had not been sanctioned by any organization.

All these demands were, however, that many elements in a many-layered strategy. They expressed first of all a marked will to get British authorities to recognize the specificity of the Muslim community. A victory in the law courts, which would have sanctioned the legitimacy of the Jamaat-i-Islami as the champion of the British Muslim community, would have totally achieved this objective. But a failure in the courts was not without its advantages either. It, in fact, made it possible to highlight the duplicity of the West, which could be accused of applying discriminatory criteria in the dispensation of justice.

In fact, its non-suit was interpreted by the Jamaat as a proof of the superiority of Islamic values.

THE INTER-STATE DIMENSION

However real its anti-West dimension, the Rushdie affair remained, even on the international level, an essentially Muslim problem. It gave the players of the main Muslim states the opportunity to continue their power struggles even if in roundabout ways. Ten years after the advent of the Islamic Republic of Iran, and the immediate aftermath of the Iran-Iraq war, the Rushdie affair became a heaven sent opportunity for the Jamaat-i-Islami and Saudi Arabia to regain the leadership of the struggle for the recognition of an Islamic identity. *The Satanic Verses* constituted one of those rare issues on which the Sunnis and the Shias were in agreement. For Saudi Arabia, which was bent on competing with Iran, the affair supplied the ideal cause to enable the Kingdom to once again appear as the champion of Islam.

It is in situations like these that the motivations for Saudi support to the Jamaat are to be found. Saudi Arabia was the first to react. The work was denounced on 8 October by *Ash-Sharq al-Awsat*, a Saudi journal published from London, and then by *Impact International*, a daily close to the Jamaat and sponsored by Saudi Arabia. Faiyazuddin Ahmad of the Islamic Foundation of Leicester was invited to Jeddah where he obtained the support of the World Muslim League to conduct a campaign against the work.[20] Thereafter, Saudi Arabia supported all the interventions of the Jamaat with regard to 'the affair'.[21]

THE RUSHDIE AFFAIR: THE FAILURE OF THE JAMAAT

In the final analysis, the Rushdie affair can be considered a failure for the Jamaat on two fronts. It was an ideological failure insofar as the Mawdudist organization proved incapable of imposing its interpretation. It was also an institutional failure in that it did not emerge stronger in any way from the debate.

In spite of the world-wide nature of the protest against *The Satanic Verses*, the Jamaat did not succeed in imposing a common interpretation as which could be taken proof of a global, a cultural Muslim commonality, transcending ethnic or national affiliations. The protests themselves highlighted two facts: the presence in each of the concerned countries[22] of a branch of the Jamaat-i-Islami[23] which was the organization through which information was transmitted and the similarity in local situations. The common point between the Indian, American, British or South African protests was essentially that those who formulated them were a minority population. What united the Muslims of Bradford with those of Delhi was the fact that both had an accusing finger pointed at them by the majority, the former on account of their ethnic origin, the latter because they have always been suspect in the collective Indian subconscious of being a fifth column working on behalf of Pakistan. In fact, apart from the organizations coming directly within the orbit of the Jamaat, there was a much greater similarity in situations rather than a commonality of interpretation, or rather, if there was a commonality of interpretation it was on account of the similarity of their situations. The Iran/ Saudi Arabia rivalry, which did not take long to emerge at the time of the Rushdie affair, gives the lie, moreover, to the idea of a global Muslim community.

The Rushdie affair was also an institutional failure for the Jamaat. On the local plane it was received with mixed feelings. Although the Muslim population of Bradford was around 14 per cent and the city has sometimes been called the 'capital of Islam in the United Kingdom', hardly a thousand people gathered for the demonstration at which Rushdie's book was burnt. Not only was the number of persons mobilized small, the campaign underlined the influence of traditional dignitaries more than that of the Jamaat. The Muslim population of the diaspora has the same feeling of cultural distancing from the Jamaat as it is confronted within Pakistan. This is clearly evident from the level of education of its members which is very much higher than that of the population to which it addresses itself. Since it is intellectually better armed, it presents itself as being more capable than traditional leadership, of being able to defend better the Muslim community against the aggressions of Western culture, but it is at the same time a victim of its rejection of popular piety. No more than in Pakistan, does it succeed in extricating itself from the social ghetto into which it has shut itself. In the case of the Rushdie affair, moreover, it showed itself incapable of obtaining from British authorities the least concession likely to give credibility to its claim to leadership of the Muslim community. It could neither obtain a ban from the courts nor the least modification of the blasphemy law from the Interior Ministry. After the *fatwa* of Ayatollah Khomeiny, it was quickly bypassed by other more radical Muslim organizations. The United Kingdom Committee on Islamic Affairs, among others, soon had competition from the Muslim Institute, which was later to become the Muslim Parliament.[24]

On the inter-state level, it hardly fared any better. The joint efforts of the Mawdudist party and the Saudi kingdom were almost futile. In spite of the enormous sums spent,[25] its mobilization of Muslim countries remained meagre and their reactions were tardy in coming. On 5 November 1988, the General Secretariat of the Organization of Islamic Conference (OIC) asked its member sates to take strong action against the publisher and the author if they refused to withdraw the work from sale, while on 21 November the Al-Azahr University declared *The Satanic Verses* blasphemous and called on forty-five Muslim states to take concerted action.[26] Only Bangladesh responded immediately to the call of the Secretariat of the Islamic Conference, followed on 22 November by Sudan. On 19 December, finally, a delegation of ambassadors of the Muslim countries represented in London called on the British Ministry of Internal Affairs to condemn *The Satanic Verses*.

No other government made any move till the *fatwa* issued by Ayatollah Khomeiny on 14 February 1989 which declared that Rushdie, being an apostate, deserved death. The Jamaat and the Saudis then found themselves trapped, overtaken by the radicalism of the head of the Iranian state, and their efforts began to look puny. They could neither oppose the *fatwa* as it would mean going back on their earlier position (and thus run the risk of losing all credibility), nor could they support it as it was not in keeping with their ideological stand. What was worse was, that they would lose credibility not only in the eyes of the Muslim Community but also in the eyes of their Western interlocutors. They were thus forced a low profile[27] and had to participate as spectators in a debate which they had themselves sparked off but in which now they had no part, the spotlight having been cornered by Iran.

On the strategic level, finally, there was complete failure on account of the divide between the Mawdudist organization and the population whose representation it wished to appropriate. Its relationship with its constituency was, from the outset, very ambiguous since its course of action, based on conflicting expectations, was full of contradictions. While the Mawdudist organization wanted, most of all, to demarcate a clear-cut cleavage between Muslim and Western cultures, the anti-Rushdie action had a completely different significance for the larger part of the community and particularly its younger elements, most of whom had a real desire for integration with British society. Caught between these basic contradictions, it was inevitable that the Jamaat's strategy would meet with failure. Far from promoting the recognition and enhanced integration of the Muslim community in Great Britain, its action only attracted increased scorn from the non-Muslim population and further increased communal tensions. This polarization could have been a gain for the Jamaat, but for that it would have been necessary that the Jamaat enjoy real legitimacy within the community, which was far from being the case. On the whole, the Jamaat was, once again, the vector of mobilization, but it was incapable of channeling it for its own benefit.

NOTES

1. Emilie René, *L'Affaire Rushdie. Protestation mondiale et communauté d'interprétation.* Les Cahiers du CERI, No. 18, 1997.
2. *Le Monde* devoted just two articles to 'the affair' before 14 February 1989, one on the demonstration in Bradford, the other on the one in Islamabad. The articles became numerous, on the other hand, after Khomeyni's *fatwa*.
3. The way *The Economist* dealt with it is symptomatic of this attitude. This British magazine chose, indeed, to ignore the scandal created by the publication of *The Satanic Verses*, making no mention of the Bradford demonstrations. It was only after the *fatwa* that it took up the whole affair, approaching it then from the angle of an inter-cultural conflict.
4. Daniel Pipes, *The Rushdie Affair: The Novel, the Ayatollah and the West,* New York: Carol Publishing Group, 1989, p. 19.
5. Ibid., p. 20.
6. M.M. Ahasan and A.R. Kidwai, *Sacrilege versus Civility: Muslim Perspectives on the Satanic Verses Affair,* Leicester: The Islamic Foundation, 1991, p. 11.
7. Ibid.
8. At the time of writing.
9. Emilie René, op. cit., p. 4.
10. It was also around this time that the Jamaat-i-Islami Pakistan tried to get closer to young labourers by creating the movement of the Pasbans.
11. Jean-Francois Clément, 'L'Affaire Rushdie', *Annuaire de l'Afrique du Nord,* Tome XXVII, 1988, Editions du CNRS, pp. 255–79, specially p. 259.
12. M.M. Ahasan and A.R. Kidwai, op. cit., p. 13.
13. Jean-Francois Clément, op. cit., p. 259.

14. Ibid.
15. *The Islamic Foundation, Objectives, Activities, Projects*, U.K., Leicester: Islamic Foundation, p. 2.
16. Mohammad-Reza Djalili, *Diplomatie islamique: stratégie internationale du Khomeynisme*, Paris: Presses Universitaires de France, 1989, p. 19.
17. The Indian Muslim community, for instance, cannot in any way be considered as a diaspora.
18. In particular, the blasphemy law. See Dominique Dhombre, 'Mahomet doit-il etre protégé par la loi britannique sur le blasphème?', *Le Monde*, 2 February 1989.
19. Daniel Pipes, op. cit., p. 20.
20. Ibid.
21. As chronicled earlier.
22. This relates to the period preceding the *fatwa* of Ayatollah Khomeyni.
23. Islamic Foundation of Leicester in Great Britain, the Islamic Circle of North America in the United States and the Youth Muslim Movement in South Africa.
24. Gilles Kepel, *A l'ouest d'Allah*, op. cit., p. 195.
25. Saudi Arabia is said to have spent some 2,50,000 pounds sterling in the single city of Bradford. Daniel Pipes, op. cit., p. 134.
26. M.M. Ahasan and A.R. Kidwai, op. cit., p. 12.
27. Saudi Arabia even tried to get the issue of *The Satanic Verses* removed from the agenda of the discussions of the OIC in March 1989, Daniel Pipes, op. cit., p. 135.

7. Conclusion: The Jamaat-i-Islami as a Factor of Destabilization

What conclusion should be drawn, at the end of this brief study, from the experiment conducted by the Jamaat in the last fifty years or so? Even before we conclude whether a 'peril', exists or not, one cardinal fact stands out: that in countries with a Muslim majority, the Jamaat has taken on a national character to the extent at least to which these states have Islamized themselves. Beyond that, however, can one talk of the existence of a 'green peril' as some assert? If there is no such 'peril' can we look forward to more promising times to come? Has the political practice of the Jamaat deflected the dogma into a more democratic direction? How are we to evaluate, finally, its capacity for the mobilization of the Muslim diaspora in Europe?

AN AMBIGUOUS RELATIONSHIP WITH DEMOCRACY

The ambiguity of its relationship with democracy certainly constitutes a major obstacle to the eventual electoral success of the Jamaat. It has to keep oscillating continuously between an ideology with totalitarian consequences and a strategy which in the end makes democracy the vector of its success and constitutes, objectively, the condition of its political survival. Consecutively, the entire history of the Jamaat-i-Islami is an attempt to overcome this contradiction. Between 1920 and 1970, its political thought, which was in effect the thought of Mawdudi, has incessantly evolved in consonance with specific historical circumstances.

In fact, the entire political history of the Jamaat is marked by this contradiction. While Western style democracy still remains hateful from the theoretical point of view, it constitutes nonetheless the condition of the political survival of the Jamaat, and its defence is the only strategy possible, as is illustrated today by its relationship with the military regime of General Musharraf.

THE TEMPTATION TO TAKE RECOURSE TO VIOLENCE

Finally, can one say that the history of the relations that the Jamaat-i-Islami has had with the Pakistani state constitute a sort of 'model' for the management of politico-religious movements? The reply to such a question would require a separate study, the history of the Jamaat being too small a base to build a model on.

Confronted with authoritarian regimes, it has seen in the fight for democracy the means of its political survival. However, it is precisely the deadlock that this type of situation results in which motivates a number of Islamist parties to make the transition to violence. The Jamaat, or more precisely its student branch, the Islami Jamiat-i-Tulabah, which unleashed terror on university campuses at one time, is also tempted to take recourse to such means. The Jamaat intervened on several occasions to attempt to rein in, though with limited success, the fervour of its young sympathizers. The participation of the Jamaat in various conflicts, and its collaboration with the army explain undoubtedly this restricted use of violence within the country. The secession of East Pakistan, the war in Afghanistan, Kashmir or the Tajikistan conflict provided outlets for the violence that the political situation of the country threatened to throw up. It provided at the same time, a means to the state machinery to co-opt the party. The key to the self-restriction of the Jamaat is to be found less in the love for democracy than in the need for participation in power in any form.

Generally speaking, the destabilizing potential of Islamist parties in a given regime is much less powerful when they are better integrated with the national political action. Examining the idea of the 'Islamist peril', Graham Fuller and Ian Lesser observe that 'where they have been particularly suppressed and persecuted . . . they have gained greater mystique, an appeal of the forbidden, a "magical" quality reflecting their ubiquitous and simplistic slogan "Al-Islam Huwwa al-Hall" (Islam is the solution). Deprived of the possibility to participate extensively in government, the Islamists have the luxury of proclaiming the "solution" without actually having to demonstrate just what their solution is to so many intractable problems.'[1] In fact, Islamism seems essentially to be the problem of failed, and above all, politically deadlocked, Muslim countries.

Conversely, the experience of Pakistan and Bangladesh shows that the inclusion of Islamist parties like the Jamaat-i-Islami in the national political systems leads to a radically different outcome. Its main characteristic is the phenomenon of 'trivialization'. As representatives in Parliament or simply as normal actors on the political scene, the Islamist parties must take a stand on real problems to which they are obliged to suggest solutions that are no less concrete. Even if their criticism of the system (corruption, social injustice, etc., problems endemic to the countries being considered here) is often sound, they do not necessarily have any miraculous solution to offer for the ills of society. Their stands are moreover, public and Islamist politicians, like all others, have to be judged on the touchstone of their actions and declarations. Hence, they are subject to the same electoral reverses as their counterparts in other parties. The game of politics, which often forces them to make compromises with their political adversaries, thus jeopardizes their claim of ideological purity.

The experiment with power conducted by the Jamaat-i-Islami Pakistan during the regime of Zia-ul-Haq was, from this point of view both revealing and disastrous. Having agreed to participate in the government even though it had condemned the coup, the Jamaat was not only incapable of bringing about the slightest reform, it was also forced to withdraw the entire team of its members from the government at the end of a few months and it ended up having to bear the opprobrium of having collaborated with the Pakistani dictator. In fact, once they have become integrated with the political scene in a normal manner, the Islamist parties begin quickly to resemble other parties and lose a good part of their attraction, as is testified by the electoral results of the Jamaat-i-Islami in Pakistan and in Bangladesh.

The question of the limits of Islamist parties when they participate in the democratic process, however, remains extant. Is democracy even today for the Jamaat a simple strategy for the conquest of power? Has it, on the contrary, been integrated into the ideological baggage of the party? One must perforce note that this baggage has hardly developed under the guidance of the successors of Mawdudi, Mian Tufail and Qazi Hussein Ahmad, more activists than ideologists. Even though the chance of a political victory by the Jamaat remains highly improbable, there is little risk of a slide towards totalitarianism. Fifty years after the creation of Pakistan, the Jamaat remains an eternal opposition party whose singularly limited social base prevents it from hoping to be anything other than a catalyst for dissent and protest.

NOTE

1. Graham Fuller and Ian Lesser, *The Geopolitics of Islam and the West*, Lahore: Vanguard Books, 1996, p. 1.

Select Bibliography

BOOKS

Ahasan, M.M. and A.R. Kidwai, *Sacrilege versus Civility: Muslim Perspectives on the Satanic Verses Affair*, Leicester: The Islamic Foundation, 1991.

Agwani, M.S., *Islamic Fundamentalism in India*, Chandigarh: Twenty-First Century India Society, 1986.

Ahmed, Ishtiaq, *The Concept of an Islamic state in Pakistan*, Lahore: Vanguard, 1991.

Bahadur, Kalim, *The Jama'at-i-Islami of Pakistan: Political Thought and Political Action*, New Delhi: Chetana Publications, 1979, p. 13.

Banuazizi, Ali and Myron Weiner, *The State, Religion and Ethnic Politics: Afghanistan, Iran and Pakistan*, Syracuse and New York: Syracuse University Press, 1986.

Bernard, J.A. and M. Pochoy, *L'ambition de l'Inde*, Paris: Fondation pour les études de défense nationale, 1988.

Borcke, Astrid, *Unforeseen Consequences of a Soviet Intervention: The Movement of the Afghans in Militant Islamism*, Koln, Bundesinstitut fur Ostewissenschatliche und Internationale Studien.

Carre, Olivier and Dumont Dumont, *Radicalismes islamiques*, Paris: l'Harmattan, 1986.

Choueiri, Yousef M., *Islamic Fundamentalism*, London: Pinter Publishers, 1990.

Djalili, Mohammed-Reza and Frédéric Grare, *Le Tadjikistan à l'épreuve de l'indépendance*, Geneva: IUHEI, 1995.

Djalili, Mohammed-Reza, *Diplomatie islamique: stratégie internationale du Khomeynisme*, Paris: Presses universitaires de France, 1988.

Fuller, Graham and Ian Lesser, *The Geopolitics of Islam and the West*, Lahore: Vanguard, 1996.

Grare, Frédéric, *Le Pakistan face au conflit afghan (1979–85): au tournant de la guerre froide*, Paris: l'Harmattan, 1997.

Kepel, Gilles, *A l'ouest d'Allah*, Paris: Le Seuil, 1994.

Kaur, Kulwand, *Pak-Afghanistan Relations*, New Delhi: Deep & Deep Publications, 1985.

Marty, Martin and Appleby Scott (ed.), *Accounting for Fundamentalisms*, Chicago and London: University of Chicago Press, 1984.

Mayer, Jean-Francois, *Religions et sécurité internationale*, Berne: Central Defence Office, December 1995.

Mawdudi, Sayyed Abul Ala, *The Economic Problem of Man and its Solution*, Delhi: Markazi Maktaba Islami, 1989.

———, *Islamic Law and Constitution*, Lahore: Islamic Publications, 9th edn., June 1986.

———, *Unity of the Muslim World*, Lahore: Islamic Publications Ltd., 1st edn., July 1967.

Muslehuddin, Muhammad, *Economics in Islam*, Lahore: Islamic Publications, 1994.

Nasr, Sayyed Vali Reza, *The Vanguard of Islamic Revolution*, London and New York: I.B.Tauris Publishers, 1994.

Nielsen, Jorgen S., *Muslims in Western Europe*, Edinburgh: Edinburgh University Press, 1992.

Pasha, A.K., *India and OIC, Strategy and Diplomacy*, New Delhi: Centre for Peace Studies, 1995.

Pipes, Daniel, *The Rushdie Affair: The Novel, the Ayatollah and the West*, New York: Carol Publishing Group, 1989, p. 19.

Ali, Rahnema (ed.), *Pioneers of Islamic Revival*, London: Zed Books, 1994.

René, Emilie, *L'Affaire Rushdie. Protestation mondiale et communauté d'interprétation*, Les cahiers du CERI, No. 18, 1997.

Rodinson, Maxime, *Islam and capitalism*, Paris, Le Seuil.

Roy, Olivier, *L'échec de l'Islam politique* Paris: Le Seuil, 1992.

———, *L'Afghanistan: Islam et modernité politiaue*, Paris: Le Seuil, 1985.

Sayyed, S.M.A., *The Myth of Authenticity: A Study of Islamic Fundamentalism*, Karachi: Royal Book Company, 1995.

Syed, Muhammad Aslam (ed.), *Islam and Democracy in Pakistan*, Islamabad: National Institute of Historical and Cultural Research, 1995.

Syed, Salahuddin Ahmad, *Foreign Policy of Pakistan: A Critical Study*, Karachi: Comprehensive Book Service, 1996.

Zvigeskaia, Irina, *The Russian Policy Debate on Central Asia*, London: The Royal Institute of International Affairs: Pinter Publishers, 1995.

ARTICLES

Anand, Vinod, 'Export of Holy Terror to Chechnya from Pakistan', *Strategic Analysis*, Vol. XXIV, No. 2, June 2000, pp. 539–51.

Aragghchi, Sayyed Abbas, 'Islamic Theo-Democrary: The Political Ideas of Abul A'La Mawdudi', *The Iranian Journal of International Affairs*, Vol. VIII, No. 4, Winter 1996–7, p. 790.

Barry, Michael, 'Kaboul: la mise à mort', *Politique internationale*, No. 64, Summer 1994, pp. 65–96.

Ceri, Peach, 'The Muslim Population of Great Britain', *Ethnic and Racial Studies*, Vol. 13, No. 3, July 1990.

Clément, Jean-Francois, 'L'Affaire Rushdie', *Annuaire de l'Afrique du Nord*, Tome XXVII, 1988, Editions du CNRS, pp. 255–79.

Gupta, Das, Jyoti Bhasu, 'Afghanistan (1979–1998)', *Asian Studies*, Vol. XVI, No. 1, January–June 1999, pp. 1–48.

Davis, Anthony, 'The conflict in Kashmir', *Jane's Intelligence Review*, Vol. 7, No. 1, 1996, pp. 40–6.

Giunchi, Elisa, 'The Political Thought of Abul A'La Mawdudi', *Il Politico*, April–June 1994, pp. 347–75.

Lavenue, Jean-Jacques, 'Sur la formation d'une internationale islamiste: la Conférence populaire islamique de Khartoum et la pensée d'Hassan El-Tourabi', *Revue de la recherche juridique*, Droit prospectif, Aix Marseille, Presses Universitaires d'Aix Marseille, No. 1, 1996, pp. 39–64.

Roy, Olivier, 'Le néo-fondamentalisme islamique ou l'imaginaire de l'oummah', *Esprit*, April 1996, pp. 80–107.

Sreedhar and Kapil Paul, 'Politics of Islamic Terrorism in West Asia: Internal and External Dimensions', *Strategic Analysis*, June 1996, Vol. XIX, No. 3, pp. 435–66.

Stobdan, P., 'Kashmir: The Key Issues', *Strategic Analysis*, Vol. XIX, No. 1, pp. 111–39.

Stern, Jessica, 'Pakistan's Jihad Culture', *Foreign Affairs*, Vol. 79, No. 6, pp. 115–26.

Yasmeen, Samina, 'Pakistan's Cautious Foreign Policy', *Survival*, Vol. 36, Summer 1994, pp. 115–33.

Index